THE
DOCTORS
GUIDE TO

Eliminating Debt

DR. CORY S. FAWCETT

The Doctors Guide to Eliminating Debt
By Dr. Cory S. Fawcett © 2016

Print ISBN: 978-1-61206-124-5
eBook ISBN: 978-1-61206-119-1

Interior and Cover Design: Fusion Creative Works, fusioncw.com
Lead Editor: Jennifer Regner

For more information, visit DrCorySFawcett.com

Published by

AlohaPublishing.com
First Printing
Printed in the United States of America

Dedication

Name _____

Address _____

_____ Date _____

℞

I dedicate this book to all physicians, dentists, pharmacists, and other healthcare professionals as you negotiate the rewarding and challenging healthcare field, and the pitfalls and potholes on the road to building a secure personal financial foundation. May you find balance in all that you do.

Signature _____ Dr. Cory S. Fawcett

Contents

Introduction

DEBT CONTROL IS THE KEY

Carrying the burden of debt has become a way of life, especially among the highly educated. It's difficult to complete eight years of school without accumulating substantial student loan debt. Once you grow accustomed to having debt, it becomes easier to accept debt in other areas of your life. Consequently, many doctors are drowning in debt. Debt is a major contributor to personal financial problems, and financial problems in turn contribute to high rates of divorce, bankruptcy, burnout, and suicide among doctors. Debt also postpones retirement dates significantly. Keeping up with the Dr. Joneses may not be healthy, since the Dr. Joneses of the world are going broke.

Even if you have lived with debt for years, don't despair—you *can* escape the quagmire and work your way back out. The financial institutions making a fortune from the interest collected on your debt have misled you. They have been transferring your wealth into their pockets for years, and all the while making it seem that they are doing you a favor. Let's face it: they are not doing you a favor!

Do they deserve your money more than you do? Did they spend years getting an education? Do they work long hours to earn it? Do they take call? Do they miss their kids' soccer games? These financial institutions *don't* deserve your money more than you do, and it's not too late to get out from under their control.

When I decided to become debt-free, something interesting happened. A weight I didn't know I was carrying seemed to lift from my shoulders, as my debt load decreased. Without the debt holding me back, I was financially able to retire at the early age of 51, despite living in a financially depressed area that provided a below-average income.

It's not difficult to become debt-free. You don't need to make great sacrifices—like living on peanut butter and Top Ramen— you merely need to make an adjustment in your attitude about how to use your money. Once the adjustment is made, it doesn't take long to get out of debt. In fact, it will take less time for you to get out of debt than it took to get the training that put you so far into debt in the first place. It may sound impossible, but it's not. Especially when you tackle the problem with the same energy you used to get through all those years of training. In reality, by redirecting how you use your money, you can leverage yourself right back out of debt and onto the path to freedom. You don't have to live in debt bondage anymore.

What's so important about being debt-free? Much, much more than the obvious. No more working extra shifts to pay the bills. No more staying home to work, while the family goes on vacation. Fewer missed school functions due to work. Your stress factor goes down and your happiness factor goes up. Without loan payments to make, your bank account grows faster. You can retire sooner. You can be free to do what you like—you can start making a difference instead of making a living. Paying cash for big-ticket items means getting them at a discount, instead of full price plus interest, which often doubles the price. The benefits of becoming a debt-free doctor are almost endless.

BECOME DEBT-FREE BY WORKING SMARTER, NOT HARDER

Working intelligently is something doctors already know how to do. Frankly, if you can understand the Krebs cycle or the clotting cascade, finances and compound interest are a breeze. Once you get a firm grasp on compound interest, you will see the importance of having it work for and not against you. While it is much easier to understand than any of the classes you took during your doctoral training, few doctors ever take the small amount of time needed to understand the basics of finance.

Life gets in the way sometimes and you never seem to find the time to devote to your financial future. You wouldn't start Mrs. Smith on chemotherapy/radiation therapy/surgical therapy for her breast cancer without a well-thought-out plan, so why do you go about spending your hard-earned money without one?

Financial wisdom is not emphasized during medical training, as there is not enough time to do it all. No one explains the true cost of purchasing a house after interest and expenses are considered. Your professors don't stress the need to start a retirement plan early. Paying off your student loans quickly to avoid thousands of dollars in interest is not covered in any rotations.

Working longer hours will make your paycheck larger, but it won't necessarily increase your wealth. Increasing your income and then following a willy-nilly spending plan causes the money to slip through your fingers. What good is all that hard work if you have nothing to show for it in the end? It's time to begin working smart in the management of your money, just like you work smart in the management of Mrs. Smith's breast cancer. Let's apply that intelligence to your finances. With the same tenacity you used to complete your doctorate, you can set in motion a financial plan to achieve wealth and freedom—but you need to start in the right direction.

If you were to take off on a flight across the country, say from San Francisco to Washington, D.C., a small and seemingly insignificant course miscalculation could ruin your trip. Pointing just five degrees in the wrong direction is not too noticeable in the first 100 yards—you're only 26 feet off course. That's less than the length of the wing, no big deal. However, by the time you get to the other side of the country, you will miss your destination by more than 200 miles. Ouch. If you were in a rocket headed to the moon, you would miss the moon by almost 21,000 miles, or almost ten times the diameter of the moon, by starting just five degrees off trajectory. Talk about being lost in space.

If you've gotten used to carrying debt without a real plan to get rid of it, you need to get back on course and work smart, so you can finish strong—even if you're getting a late start. Now is the earliest you can start any new project. You can't go back and do it over, no matter how much you wish you could. But it isn't too late; get started now, make the proper course corrections, and you can improve your financial position and eliminate your debt. Then, ten years from now, you won't look back and wish you had done it differently. The earlier you make the correction, the smaller the trajectory change will be.

Once you know better,
you can do better.

When I was in medical school, I plotted out a plan to retire at age 50. I discussed my plan with an older doctor whom I respected. He told me it was impossible. I could never save enough money to retire so early. I didn't let his statement detract from my plan. I later discovered my original plan did not take into account managing my debt; it concentrated only on managing my savings.

I didn't realize the important role debt plays in the journey to early retirement. It can be a deal breaker! Consequently, I got a little off track when I first started earning the *big bucks* and fell $500,000 deeper into debt. It took six years for me to recover from that detour and eliminate my debt. I had a plan, I followed it, and I ended up right where I wanted to be, even with my little detour. This book is about what I learned from that journey—and how you can do it too, even if you get a little off course.

I was actually 51 years old when I retired from my general surgery practice and began working on a part-time basis, providing call relief to solo general surgeons in rural critical access hospitals. Had I not been debt-free, I couldn't have retired from practice so early. Now I can work because I like it, and not because I need to make a living. You can too, even if you're a little off track—and you've taken the first step by reading this book. Make your plan to join me as a debt-free doctor and become free to live life on your terms.

The person who says it cannot be done should not interrupt the person who is doing it.

— Chinese Proverb

Chapter 1

MY DEBT-FREE JOURNEY

Back in 1996, I was three years out of residency and a partner in a general surgery practice in rural Grants Pass, Oregon. Carolyn, my wife, had stopped working as a corporate accountant so she could stay home and raise our boys, Brian and Keith, ages four and two. We were loving life with our 4-bedroom, 2-bath house on three-quarters of an acre, a few blocks from the hospital. We had a good income, a motorhome, and a time-share condominium, and we took some very nice vacations. Tagging along with us was nearly $500,000 of debt.

I went to medical school on a Navy scholarship and graduated with only $18,000 in student loans, so where did the $500,000 of debt come from? Many doctors from my era were entering residency with a large amount of debt, some exceeding $200,000. My little $18,000 student loan debt seemed to put me well ahead of the game. When my income increased after residency, so did my ability to spend and borrow. There was the time-share condominium, my third of the surgical practice and office building, a 34-foot motorhome, our first house, and a piece of property to build our future dream home.

The debt we accumulated seemed very manageable on my income. Since having lots of debt seemed normal, I didn't take any special notice of the situation. We were keeping up with the Dr. Joneses. Carolyn, though, was beginning to have other thoughts about our debt load. She worried about how she would make those payments if, for some reason, my income were to stop.

One day she showed me an advertisement for a book called *Debt-Free and Prosperous Living* by John Cummuta (Debt-Free Prosperous Living, Inc.). Getting out of debt was on her mind but was not on my radar yet. Certainly *we* didn't need this information, but I knew someone who did. His family was struggling financially and debt was a big part of the problem. We decided to buy him this book as a gift. At the time, I didn't realize how much my wife was hoping I'd get the hint.

When the book arrived, I read it in preparation for any questions he might have. I learned for the first time about the snowball method for eliminating debt, which I will explain in more depth in chapter 6. A quick synopsis: take the amount of available extra money you have and apply it to one debt, in addition to the regular payment; when the first debt is paid off, roll the extra money plus the first debt's regular payment over onto the next debt, and so on as each one gets paid off. The payments keep getting larger, like a snowball rolling down a hill. When I reached the paragraph stating nearly everyone could get out of debt within five to seven years—including their home mortgage—I was shocked. My first thought was, *that's impossible.* There was no way a 30-year mortgage could be paid off in only seven years, and at the same time pay off all the other debt. If that were possible, everyone would be doing it. Nevertheless, the concept kept gnawing at me. Was it possible? Could it really be done?

The chart below summarizes my debts at the time.

MY BEGINNING DEBT

Loan	Principal	Monthly Payment	Interest	Interest Rate
Student loan	$ 3,164	$ 61	$ 8	3.00%
Motorhome	27,229	367	199	8.75%
Land, future homesite	52,500	1,100	460	10.50%
Office bldg., partner 1	58,552	1,111	512	10.50%
Office bldg., partner 2	58,552	1,111	512	10.50%
Home	127,717	1,280	745	7.00%
Total	327,714	5,030	2,436	
AR office	163,825	2,278	-	0.00%
Grand Total	$ 491,539	$7,308	$2,436	

My student loan balance was $3,164, after eight years of payments. There was the motorhome and the land we purchased for our future dream home. I was buying my share of the office building from each of my two partners, and we had a home mortgage. The other figure was the purchase of the accounts receivable (AR), which came out of my share of the practice income and was distributed to my partners before I was paid.

Looking over my numbers, I didn't see how it could be possible to pay it all off so quickly. I decided I would set out to prove it could not be done. It might be possible for the average Joe to pay off his debt that fast, but not the typical doctor who carries an enormous debt load. I put my actual figures in a spreadsheet and ran through the snowball plan. The calculations confirmed I could be debt-free in three and a half years! After my wife double-checked the figures, I knew it must be true.

If we could be debt-free in about three and a half years, we were going to give it a shot. That was far better than the 30-year plan we were on. An important crossroads was in front of us—a fork in the road that could drastically change our financial future. We took the road less traveled. We kept the book, ordered another one for my friend, and set out on our journey to become debt-free.

Since we lived with a budget already, we were easily able to calculate how much money we could apply each month as extra payments to get us out of debt: $3,900. It made sense to pay off my remaining student loans the first month; I had a hang-up about it, though. I was so fixated on the 3% interest rate, in relation to the other debts, that I never saw the wisdom of eliminating my final student loan with a single payment.

We decided to tackle the land loan first. I wanted to go for the higher interest loan, even though two other loans could have been paid off quicker. Thanks to using some savings and our tax refund, we paid off our first debt about six months into our journey—several years ahead of schedule. In fact, we did it five months ahead of our prediction. That was the real turning point on our journey, the moment we knew this would actually work. Up until then I was still a bit skeptical, but Carolyn was all in. Now I was all in as well. Besides the weight that was lifted when the debt was gone, there was a freedom in no longer having to make payments on the loan—no more writing checks, labeling envelopes, and licking stamps. Today, that might be one less payment to make online.

I began telling everyone who would listen, how they too could become debt-free. I thought everyone would want to jump on the bandwagon with me. That was not the case.

Most of the people I talked to were skeptical, the same way I felt initially. I told them they didn't have to make great sacrifices. They only needed to change some habits and do things a little differently. Once the debt-free goal is set, decisions are made with the new goal in mind. One skeptical doctor told me, "Yeah, right, and you can lose weight without dieting or exercise." He never became debt-free, but we did.

You miss 100% of the shots you don't take.

– Wayne Gretzky

One nurse accepted this advice and began the journey with us. She made her final house payment within a few months of our final house payment. This will work for almost everyone, because your income determines the maximum debt load you can handle. The higher the income, the higher the sustainable debt. You can't compare your debt to anyone else's, unless your income is similar. Just as my nurse friend couldn't handle the same debt load as I could with my larger income, I couldn't handle the debt load Bill Gates could with his larger income. Since most people's debt is usually in proportion to their income, almost everyone is about a half-dozen years from being debt-free. One caveat: the lower the prevailing interest rate, the more you can borrow on your income, and the longer it will take to pay back.

It seemed everyone could come up with an excuse to avoid paying down debt ahead of schedule. Those with high income and high debt often used the excuse that they had too much debt to pay it off quickly, but it would work for the average Joe because he has less debt. Those with low income and low debt often said they had too little income to pay off their debt early, but it would work for doctors because they had a higher income. Anyone can find an excuse.

I was surprised to find such opposition to becoming debt-free. I thought it would be a no-brainer, but I learned that since debt is ingrained into our way of thinking, anyone teaching otherwise is looked on with suspicion.

During what was to be a three-and-a-half-year journey down debt-free lane, we took a few detours. Sometimes life happens, and we shouldn't become so rigid we can't bend a little in the wind. We bought a bigger house, joined a partnership to build a surgery center, and replaced both cars—which were holdouts from residency. The new house pushed our total debt up to $640,000 and we paid cash for the rest. Those detours lengthened our journey a bit, and we paid our final mortgage payment less than six years after making the decision to become debt-free. In October of 2001, we joined a growing minority of Americans who actually have title to their homes. No more bank. No more payments. We were debt-free! Two months later, the final transfer was made to my partners for my accounts receivable purchase, and my monthly gross income went up by $2,278.

We found it much easier to cover unexpected expenses during our journey than before we started. When we decided to replace a car, we simply stopped making the extra payments for a few months and quickly accumulated the cash for the car. If the transmission went out, we paid for it with that month's extra payment and did not borrow. The new purchase simply delayed our plan by a month instead of putting us further into debt.

MY ACTUAL SNOWBALL EFFECT

Loan	Beginning Principal	Required Payment	Snowball Payment	Predicted Payoff Date	Actual Payoff Date
Beginning extra payment			$ 3,900		
Land, future homesite	52,500	1,100	5,000	12/96	7/96
Motorhome	27,229	367	5,367	5/97	12/97
Student loan	3,164	61	5,428	6/97	2/97
Office bldg., partner 1	58,552	1,111	6,539	3/98	3/98
Office bldg., partner 2	58,552	1,111	7,650	10/98	3/98
Initial home	127,717	1,280	8,930	11/99	11/97
Later home	287,200	2,703	11,633	1/00	10/01
AR office	$163,825	$ 2,278		12/01	12/01

The above chart shows the plan we established with our $3,900 extra payment each month, beginning in February 1996, and the predicted payoff dates. The chart also shows the actual dates we made each final loan payment. Sometimes we were ahead of the prediction and sometimes we were behind, but we continued to make steady progress.

Once we became free from our debt, we couldn't imagine going back to the old way of life. The freedom of not having a mortgage to pay each month is unbelievably rewarding.

Our new budget allowed for increased investing. We formed an LLC for real estate investing and began to buy apartment complexes. Each of them had a mortgage, but the rental income covered the mortgage with money left over. We then used those profits, which were not needed for our personal budget, as well as a portion of our snowball payment, to accelerate the mortgage payoff for the LLC. Thus, we applied the same principle we used in our personal life to make our real estate business debt-free as soon as possible.

My wife and I decided to make every effort to remain debt-free in our personal budget. Today, our LLC still has some real estate debt, and we are paying it down as quickly as we can. Without personal debts to pay, money accumulates very rapidly. Our future purchases—cars, motorhomes, vacations, and toys—are made by saving first and paying cash. We have abided by the philosophy, "If we can't pay cash for something, we can't afford it." We are living a very good life using this method, and you can too.

THE IMPACT OF NOT HAVING A MORTGAGE UPON RETIREMENT

The $365,000 house we purchased during our debt-free journey had a $3,067 per month payment (the $2,703 payment listed in the table was only principal and interest on the loan; the full payment had property tax as well). After paying off the house, if we were to invest the original monthly payment into our retirement plan over the 24 years remaining on the mortgage, assuming an average 8% return, we would generate a balance of $2,658,001 at the end of our original 30-year plan. Making withdrawals at 4% a year would give us a gross income of $106,320 a year, from the money we would have paid in mortgage payments. Investing the house payments and having compound interest working in our favor would position us to not only own our home at retirement, but we would have an additional $2.6 million in the bank.

We discovered another interesting result of having no mortgage payment. Had we kept on the conventional path, we would have probably refinanced the house several times and extended the term for another 30 years each time, leaving us with a house payment when I reached retirement age. Making a monthly house payment of $3,067 during retirement requires a net income of $36,804 each year from investments. Allowing for taxes paid on that income, that figure becomes about $50,000 a year. Withdrawing the recommended 4% each year would require a retirement nest egg of $1.25 million, just to cover the house payment.

Let that sink in a bit. Covering the mortgage on my $365,000 house (a $287,200 mortgage) requires $1.25 million in savings. Put another way, removing the house payment lowered our retirement plan needs by $1.25 million. Wouldn't it be far wiser to pay off the $287,200? That's what we thought. Removing our debt and putting those payments to work for us put me in a position to retire from the grind and do medicine the way I wanted at age 51. If I still had the house payment, I could not have retired when I did.

> Whatever the financial goal, it's much easier to accomplish when we position ourselves on the receiving side of interest.

NEW ATTITUDE ABOUT DEBT

I would not have been able to start down a path to become debt-free if I had not developed a new attitude toward debt. Maybe an example that puts debt in a new light will help you move closer to the debt-free attitude that took hold of me.

Maybe if you could see debt as a disease, you would feel differently about allowing it into your life.

Healthcare providers are trained to think about disease using a reproducible and standardized method. It has a cause, distinctive characteristics, ways to prevent it, methods of treatment, possible recurrence, and many other aspects. When you look at debt in the same manner as you look at diseases, you get a different perspective on its effect in your life.

The truth is, debt is not your friend—it's a disease. When sifting through the mail, watching television, or reading magazines, you get the impression that debt is no big deal. In fact, you are led to believe that when someone offers you credit, they are doing you a big favor. They are helping you get something you want now without that awful wait. All it takes is a few easy monthly payments. These ads are everywhere.

Always remember when someone is offering you credit, they are not *giving* you anything. They are setting you up to begin a wealth transfusion from your wallet to theirs, while making it look like they are doing you a favor. If you look closely at the effects of debt on your family, you can begin to see the disease characteristics. It causes depression, anxiety, fighting, divorce, and even death from suicide when no other alternative presents itself.

Put on your white coats and take a new look at debt through the eyes of a clinician. Let's start by giving the new disease a name:

malignant credit carcinoma

Prevalence: Has been increasing during the last century. A small percentage of the population had a home mortgage in the 1920s, and a small percentage don't have one today. No one had credit card debt in the 1940s, and today among the households carrying a balance, the average exceeds $15,000. Almost never found in the pediatric population. Seen more often in developed countries.

Symptoms: Irritability, sleeplessness, fear, need to shop, stress, burnout, and suicidal ideations.

Signs: Unpaid credit card balance, car payments, arguments over finances, calls from collection agencies, past due notices, robbing Peter to pay Paul, needing to borrow money from friends and family, juggling payments, second mortgages.

Etiology: Greed, major health problems, keeping up with the Dr. Joneses, frequently buying new cars, student loans, misuse of credit cards, easy monthly payments, unpaid taxes, impulse buying, and many more.

Genetics: Incomplete penetrance. Often passed on through multiple generations. If the parents have it, high probability of the children having it also.

Infectious: Probably airborne and quite contagious, often transferred friend to friend, especially at the mall or in the driveway while looking at a friend's new car, boat, or motorhome.

Tumor Characteristics: Usually found on the back or shoulders and feels like a heavy weight. Will not stop growing until its propagating element—borrowing money—is stopped. Not noticed by the patient in its early stages.

Treatment: Early plastic surgery on credit cards: cut them up. Stop borrowing money. Accelerated payments on loans. Search out lower interest rates. Participate in loan forgiveness programs. Usually takes five to seven years to treat.

Prognosis: Good if permanent lifestyle changes are made.

Complications: Fighting with spouse, divorce, bankruptcy, loss of sleep, depression, suicide, irritability, malaise, aches and pains, migraines, debtabetic neuropathy (explained later), Alzheimer's debtmentia (explained later), and burnout.

As you can see, it is easy to look at debt in the typical disease template, and when doing so it is harder to tolerate it in your life. The good news is the disease is very responsive to therapy. Fortunately, we already know the cure for malignant credit carcinoma, and it produces miraculous results. The biggest step in treating this disease is a keen awareness of the problem and a change in attitude about tolerating its presence. This sounds like a bad disease and one we should strive to avoid. Unfortunately, that is not what is happening.

I spent many years thinking debt was a normal part of life. I no longer live by that philosophy. After becoming debt-free and seeing a different way, I have found such a remarkable new life that I want to share what I've learned with everyone who will listen.

THE DEBT-FREE ADVANTAGE

Being debt-free has many advantages. When you have no debt, you have much less stress. You don't worry about making the mortgage payment. When the family is going on vacation, you don't have to stay home and work to keep paying the overhead. When the hospital tells you about the new changes in your contract, you can have the courage to say no. When the government mandates new changes for your practice, you will have the money to implement them. When your children need braces, you have the money. Because you are not paying this year for last year's indulgences, more money is available.

You have more flexibility. You can have more fun. You can take time off. You can stop seeing a certain type of patient you don't like or that causes you anxiety. You can stop doing a procedure you don't enjoy. You can take more vacations. You can take a day off during the week, every week. If you want a new toy, you can have it and pay cash. You can pay for your vacation before you leave. You can drive any car you want. You can go anywhere you want. There is great freedom in having no debts and money in the bank. When a great investment opportunity comes across your desk, you can take it. If you want to retire early, you can. If your spouse wants to stay home to raise the kids, you can afford it.

There are many more open doors for those with no debt and available money in the bank than there are for those with crushing debt and nothing in the bank. If you have to borrow money to do everything, many things will be beyond your grasp. I have lived both with personal debt and without personal debt and I can assure you, debt-free is better.

You can become debt-free.

PASSING IT FORWARD

Becoming debt-free totally changed my life. I felt freer without the bills hanging over me. I had more money to do fun things. I had more money to invest. I had more money to give to church and charity. I had the freedom to stop doing the surgeries I didn't like, which improved my practice and my happiness in the office. I had more free time. In short, my quality of life went up a few notches.

I wanted to pass that on to others. If becoming debt-free had such an impact on me, it should have a similar impact on others. I began to talk to anyone who would listen. My wife and I started teaching a Bible study on money management through Crown Financial Ministries. Debt became the topic of discussion over the operating table and in the cafeteria. Nurses would pass me in the halls and give me a high five, telling me they were so excited to have paid off their second credit card and wanted to thank me for the advice. I spoke about finances to various organizations. My church asked me to give sermons on finance.

Sometimes I would come home late, and my wife would ask what took so long. I would say, someone asked me how to get out of debt and I lost track of time. She knows very well what happens when I start talking about getting out of debt and the excitement I pass on to others.

Eventually I was financially able to retire from my practice. I wasn't ready to merely hang out at the clubhouse after a great game of golf. I still had many productive years left—I just didn't want to work so hard anymore. I started working part-time, giving call coverage relief to doctors working solo in critical access hospitals. This gave me something important to do, and I could still use the skills I acquired during twenty years of private practice as a general surgeon. My passion, though, was moving away from surgery and into teaching finance to medical professionals. With my newly acquired free time, I was looking into other options.

I found a way to combine both medicine and finance into one place and started a business called Prescription for Financial Success, helping other doctors attain the financial freedom I had, and especially helping them become debt-free. I found a way to turn my avocation into a vocation. Then my idea of writing a book turned into a series of books, to pass on my message to even more doctors. You are proof of its effectiveness, as you are now reading book two in the series.

Now I'm living my dream of teaching financial concepts to doctors and helping them regain control of their lives. I hope you will enjoy the fruits of my labor.

So much for my story. Let's move on to the story of how you will conquer your debt.

Chapter 2

BALANCE

All of life is a balancing act. Driving a car is a delicate balance between the gas, the brake, and the steering wheel. Too much brake and we go nowhere. Too much gas and we can't control the car. Too much left turn and we end up in the ditch. When we attain balance between all these controls, we arrive at our destination unscathed and in record time.

Finding balance with your finances is similar to driving a car. You must learn to balance your debt (the past) with your savings (the future) and your desire to spend money for your life now (the present). When you get out of balance, you end up in the ditch. Every time you make a decision to do something with your money, it also affects the other areas. If you buy a new suit now, that money is not available to pay off debt, nor is it available to save for your future. You must strike a balance to stay out of the ditch.

If you don't understand the concept of balance, you may be soured on the idea of becoming debt-free. Does becoming debt-free conjure up a vision of using all your finances to pay off debt and leaving nothing for the present and the future? This would be like driving with the brake on; you won't get very far. Putting all your effort into only one of the three areas of your finances—past, present, or future—will not work. No one can drive a car using only the brake and ignoring the gas pedal and the steering wheel. You would never consider driving that way. Yet, most people have that image when they contemplate paying off their debt: all brake.

Instead, think of the decision to eliminate debt as a promise to stop driving recklessly—to drive within the speed limit, stay between the lines, and follow the GPS to your destination. That's called driving responsibly, and that's how you need to use your money. Not spending it on whatever you want now, without regard to your income or other commitments. Not buying a house because you love it, but buying the house that fits your income and your needs. The right balance is what you need to reach the financial destination of your dreams.

A second illustration might help to demonstrate the balance you need to manage your finances best in your specific situation. Picture your finances as a water jug with three spigots. Your earned income continually fills the jug, and the spigots represent the outflow of money to meet your financial past, present, and future needs. The level of water in the jug is your reserve. The outflow must not exceed the inflow or your jug will run empty, and you will be bankrupt.

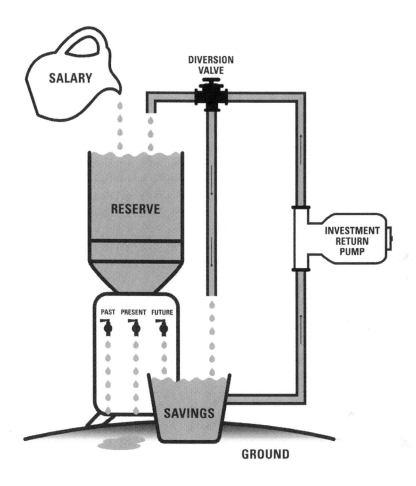

FINANCIAL BALANCE

The past is your debt; you borrowed money and agreed to pay it back. What flows out of this spigot falls on the ground and is lost. How you decide to repay this debt affects the amount of money you have to spend in the present and invest for the future. If you keep adding debt, the increased interest on the debt empties the jug faster—making it necessary to dial back one or both of the other spigots or find ways to increase your income to put more in the jug. If you don't open the other two spigots full bore, you can pay off the debt faster. Once you pay off the debt and can close that spigot, you can open the other two spigots wider without running dry. Your goal is to close the debt spigot as quickly as possible.

The present is your lifestyle. What flows out this spigot is also lost. How lavishly or simply you live will affect your ability to pay off the past and invest for the future. If you open the lifestyle spigot too wide, you can't pay off the debt or invest adequately in the future without running dry. However, this spigot cannot be turned off completely, as you will always have living expenses such as food, clothing, shelter, and other necessities of life.

The future is your investing. This spigot does not drain onto the ground but into another jug, the savings jug. The income (interest/dividends/etc.) produced by this second jug goes into a pump and is either put back into the savings jug to fill it faster or is pumped into the first jug as passive income. If you can shut off the debt spigot and your savings jug can produce enough passive income to keep up with the lifestyle spigot's flow, you can retire and stop pouring earned income into the jug. If you neglect the savings jug early on, you will find yourself struggling in the future (during retirement) to keep your jug from running dry. With no reserves in the savings jug to create a passive income, you may be unable to retire. Don't end up with an empty savings jug.

Your debt repayment, spending, and investing choices will not drain the jug dry if you balance their outflow with the inflow. You will be able to keep the jug partly full as a reservoir for use in case of drought or unexpected water requirements. Your short-term savings is represented by the depth of the water in the main jug. How you choose to handle debt is the key to balancing your finances. All three aspects—past, present, and future—are important and each has an effect on the others. Too much debt and you can't thrive or invest. Too much partying now and you might drown in your debt or have no retirement future. Too much investing and you don't have any fun now and the interest on your debt will soak up too much of your wealth.

THE PAST

By the time you complete your training, you've spent many years accumulating debt on the premise that you would pay it back in the future. When the future arrives, it's easy to forget now is the time you were going to pay back that debt. It's very human to want to spend in the present and postpone paying the debt. When you add more debt in the present, the debt spigot starts flowing faster than the other two. Eventually the debt will become overwhelming and bankruptcy could be looming ahead. The water jug is running dry.

I am frequently asked the following question: "Should I pay off my student loans before I put money aside to invest in the stock market?" The person asking this *quick and simple question* is looking for a yes or no answer. The problem I am faced with is there is not enough information in the question to give a proper answer. Therefore, I say, *it depends.*

It depends on how the debt (past) compares to the present and the future. If you are drowning in debt and struggling each month to get by, then the first step must be to restore a workable balance. There are more than financial ramifications to overwhelming debt. Arguments over finances are the leading cause stated for divorce. Burnout and suicide are both linked to overwhelming debt. In this situation, all efforts need to go toward debt elimination, until balance and breathing room are re-established—even to the extreme of stopping all 401(k) or other retirement investing until balance is restored. In the investment world, that's heresy. You should be maxing out your 401(k), shouldn't you? Not if you are seriously out of balance and at risk of drowning in debt.

This decision should be made with the same urgency you use when approaching a code blue. You cannot be concerned about the patient's cholesterol level until you restore his circulation. All efforts go into CPR until you have a surviving patient.

Then, tomorrow you can think about lowering the patient's cholesterol for his long-term overall health. You must save his life first; everything else can wait.

If, on the other hand, debt is not overwhelming your finances, then you can take a more balanced approach. You may be able to pay down debt ahead of schedule and at the same time make this year's maximum retirement plan contribution. Most doctors are in a position to do both, if their lifestyle spending (present) is also in balance.

Overemphasis on debt repayment leaves too little for the present and the future. Underemphasis, though, causes the same effect from runaway interest payments.

THE PRESENT

Nothing messes up a good plan for a balanced financial life more than overspending in the present budget. It's human nature, but it's like a siren call luring us to our death—we spent so many years under financial restraint, when it's lifted we tend to go overboard. We buy too much house, too many toys, and quickly get out of balance.

If residents learn to reach a balance before getting their big pay raise as attendings, they can avert many financial problems. They can start out with a sound financial plan that includes balancing debt repayment and retirement planning from the outset. The lifestyle they choose would fit in and not tip them out of balance.

All too often, I meet with a doctor who didn't start on a balanced path and, years later, realizes retirement is not within his grasp. The decisions needed at this later point are a lot harder than those made earlier. The course correction needed when you are over Atlanta on your journey to D.C. is much larger than what's needed if you are over Denver. Buying a house that fits your spending plan is much easier than selling a house you are accustomed to but cannot afford. Don't despair if this is you—a late correction is still better than no correction at all.

Balance must be restored before financial peace can be achieved. Overemphasis on the present—spending too freely—leaves nothing for the past or future. Underemphasis may lead to a pauper's lifestyle; spouses aren't too hip on that—and life is too short to not enjoy the journey. Doctors earn a good living and deserve to live a fun and fulfilled life. Isn't that why you work in the first place? To make a living? Just don't get so far out of balance that it negatively affects your life.

THE FUTURE

The future is in your savings, investment portfolio, and retirement plan. It's money you have set aside, that you would have otherwise spent in the present, to live better when you're older and no longer desire or are no longer able to earn an income.

Delayed gratification is not a foreign concept to doctors; we all did it for years during training. What you accumulate in your portfolio will be the major factor in determining how well you live in your retirement years. Will you be traveling or sitting at home? A small trade-off in the present will boost your future well-being immensely.

When interest is compounding in your favor, time is your best friend. The longer it grows, the more you have. With this in mind, you need to start saving yesterday. A $12,000 investment today at 8% interest will earn $960 this year. Fast-forward 40 years when your portfolio has grown to $3.5 million, and the return is $280,000 in one year. Delaying the start of your investing by one year would mean missing that $280,000 final year payment. One year makes a big difference.

Understanding this concept makes it easier to think beyond the dollar amount of the investment check. The $12,000 investment now does not mean you will have an extra $12,000 to live on when you are retired. A one-year delay isn't $12,000 less you'll have 40 years from now, it is $280,000 less, since the delay only gave you 39 years in the portfolio. The 40th-year interest payment is missing.

I began investing for retirement the first year I started earning a steady, year-round income, during my first year of residency. I maxed out the 403(b) deferred compensation plan offered to residents, as well as my IRA and my wife's IRA. I did not want to miss each year's opportunity. There is no chance to catch up on missed tax-advantaged investments like an IRA. Each year carries a maximum deposit.

Underemphasis on the future may cost you a comfortable retirement by not having enough money in your retirement plan when you need it.

Overemphasis on future investing leads to missing out in the present. If you skip the trip to Paris to add more money to a retirement account that already has more than you need, you're missing out on the present—you're out of balance.

Finding the balance between these three financial elements is key to your overall financial peace and tranquility. Most financial advisors only talk about finding a balance within the investment leg of this trio—getting the right mix of cash, stocks, and bonds, and rebalancing each year. While this is important to good investing, a much more important concept is finding the right balance between debt repayment, lifestyle spending, and retirement investing, and reassessing it each year to maintain the balance.

This concept is critical to enjoying life to its fullest in every phase of your life: learning years (school), earning years (working), and burning years (retirement). Playing your cards right all along the way will maximize your benefit in each of these seasons of your life, and in the immortal words of Spock, you will "live long and prosper."

ACHIEVING BALANCE

The first step toward regaining control of your financial car is to plan your trip. You need a map to get to any destination you've never visited before. With the right map, you can go anywhere. Begin by setting some goals. Once you have a destination in mind, you can figure out how to get there.

What are your financial goals? Five million dollars in the retirement account? Write it down. Retirement at age 55? Owning a beautiful house on the lake? No more home mortgage? Whatever your goals are, if you do not write them down, you are unlikely to achieve them. Think of this as the index for the map of your financial life. When you want to find something on the map, first look at the index. Do this to map out your financial future.

Once you have a destination, you can determine the price tag. Once you know the price, you can map out a plan to get there. That plan is called a spending plan.

Most doctors think of budget (or spending plan) as a bad word. No one likes to budget, but it's your road map to financial success. Everyone has to work within a limited amount of income. There is a ceiling. When resources are limited, they must be allocated for best use. You can allocate them willy-nilly and hope to get what you want—somewhat like driving on whatever road you feel like going down, and hoping to get to Disneyland. You'll never make it. Or, you can allocate your resources purposely as you move toward your goals.

Your income must exceed your expenses. You will only know this for sure if you make a spending plan. The difference between income and expense is what you can use to achieve your goals. If your expenses exceed your income, you will probably never reach your goals.

If there are things you want to achieve, you will only get them by planning to get them. Make a spending plan and identify those things you want your money to do for you. If you have a retirement date in mind, plot that out. You know how much money you have available. You know how much time you have to get there. You have an estimate of the interest rate you can work with. Plot a course to get there and don't be surprised when it actually happens. After all, you planned it that way.

Take a moment right now to establish some financial goals. You can establish many types of goals, like health, fitness, family, and others. For now, concentrate on the financial area of goal setting. The goals must be very specific, such as pay off the car. They must have a deadline, such as pay off the car in eighteen months. They must also be realistic. Using these guidelines, fill in the following chart, or something like it, to start establishing some financial goals now.

FINANCIAL GOALS

GOAL	COST	TARGET DATE	MONTHLY SAVINGS TO ACHIEVE

Chapter 3

SYMPTOMS AND CAUSES OF DEBT ACCUMULATION

When I carried $500,000 of debt and had no goal to pay it off, my debt load was actually climbing. Debt has become the norm—and since I was doing what everyone else was doing, I thought nothing of it. If I wanted something big, like my motorhome, I would buy it. If I didn't have the money for it, I would borrow it. After being debt-free became a goal, the attitude in our house changed.

To illustrate this, one day we came home to find our house had been burglarized. Among the stolen items was my bicycle. Neighborhood rides with the family were part of our fun time; my bike needed replacing for this to continue. I suggested replacing my wife's bike as well, so we would have a matching set. She asked me, "Are we debt-free yet?" I said no. She said she could ride her old bike until we were debt-free.

Here I was, ready to spend extra money for something we really didn't need. We were doing fine with the old bike yesterday, so it could wait until we were debt-free. There was no sacrifice in continuing to use the old bike. Mostly, this was an attitude change more than a sacrifice. Not replacing my bike would have been a sacrifice, as it would have ended a family activity.

When debt-free becomes your goal, you think about things a little differently. Suddenly, your four-year-old car is not too old yet. Suddenly, a vacation to Pismo Beach in southern California is every bit as nice as a vacation to Waikiki Beach in Hawaii, and about one-third the price. Both are nice vacations, but one gets you debt-free a lot quicker. It is a matter of priority, not sacrifice. It is not a sacrifice to stop buying new stuff for a while. When your debt is eliminated, you can buy all the new stuff you want, as long as you pay cash.

We've become numb to debt.

DESENSITIZATION

The high-pitched wail of the pneumatic saw cutting through the tibia and the little bits of tissue the blade flung onto the surgeon's gown were not enough to get to me the first time I saw a surgery, during my senior year in high school. It was the smell. Sliding down the wall in the corner of the operating room, wondering if lunch would stay put, I began to question my career choice. Certainly no respectable doctor would almost pass out at the sights and smells of the operating room. No one else in the room was sitting on the floor.

Eight years later, by the end of medical school, those horrifying things no longer bothered me. Blood, guts, and mucous didn't faze me anymore. I could assist my mentors with surgery and run off for lunch between cases. What had transformed a pale, withered lump in the corner of the operating room into a confident new doctor, heading off to a general surgery residency? I had become desensitized. Repeated exposure had transformed the grossly abnormal into the routine.

Wikipedia's definition of desensitization: The diminished emotional responsiveness to a negative or aversive stimulus after repeated exposure to it.

Even the greatest of surgeons had difficulty in the beginning. When a scalpel cuts through skin, it seems as if it's your own flesh being divided. Later on, after repeatedly witnessing things the average Joe would consider horrific, you don't even bat an eye.

Think back to a few months before your high school graduation. Standing in the kitchen with Mom and Dad, reading your first financial aid/student loan package from Dream College University. Is your hand shaking from the opportunity or in fear of the looming debt? You begin to wonder:

How will I ever pay it off?

How much will the interest total?

Can I afford this?

It's a little scary, taking on debt for the first time. Maybe even horrifying.

You conquered the fear and took the plunge, joining the ranks of other Americans in debt. When the sophomore financial aid package arrived, it was a little easier to tack on a new loan. After all, nothing bad happened with the last one. Some big dude with a bat didn't show up to break your legs for not making any payments. The bank wasn't sending any nasty letters. Everyone was saying it would be easy to pay it off after graduation, when the big bucks would be rolling in.

So you did it again, adding the next student loan to the debt pile, and still nothing bad happened. Each year it got easier and easier to add more debt. You gradually became desensitized to the debt. Something horrible, initially, had become acceptable.

Fast-forward to the final year in medical school. Eight years of *add it to my debt and I'll pay it later* have passed. It was so easy to add more debt the eighth year. What will it matter if you borrow a little bit more?

If you take a moment to reflect on your borrowing years, you realize how it happened so gradually. You became so numb to the idea of debt, it meant nothing to you anymore. For eight years, you added to it and nothing happened. Life went on, and you kept getting what you wanted, always thinking it would be easy to pay later. This laissez-faire attitude sets you up to make some bad decisions.

When the real estate agent talks you into looking at a much more expensive house than you were considering, taking on the extra debt is no big deal. Debt is nothing, just toss it on the pile. When the car salesperson shows you the proper choice for a doctor, he can easily convince you to drive away in your dream car with those "small" monthly payments. Debt is nothing, just toss it on the pile. When you drive by the RV lot and see the perfect motorhome, you're sure you can handle the payments. You've not had any trouble—yet. Debt is nothing, just toss it on the pile.

Sales representatives see a doctor as a big fish, a whale, or an easy mark—and they believe you have poor investment knowledge, high income, and high debt tolerance. That's why you get so many cold calls from investors, salespeople, and brokers.

They believe you make a lot of money and are not afraid to borrow even more.

Only after you begin to face the consequences of piling on all this debt, do you realize what a monster you have created. When you reach the point where the easy monthly payments are not so easy anymore, you begin to think about debt in a new light—but now it's too late. You already owe the money. You made the deal. You signed the papers. You are hooked like a Chinook salmon at the end of a fishing line.

Early in the twentieth century, consumer debt was uncommon. If you didn't have the money, you didn't buy the product. You had to save first and buy later, if you didn't spend the money on something else while you were saving. Then, merchants realized they could sell a lot more if people didn't have to come up with the cash today. You could get it now and pay for it later—over time, with interest. No store owner wanted to risk the possibility that you would blow your money in someone else's store, so they began to extend store credit.

In 1950, the current concept of the credit card was born. It became possible to effectively have store credit in lots of stores, all on one bill. This concept expanded over the years, and now almost everything can be bought on credit. Most people today believe it is not possible to buy a car without having a car payment. Society has grown accustomed to credit. If we were to stop using it, many industries would fold, because their sales are completely dependent on credit. If people had to save up the money first, most would never be able to buy a new car at today's prices.

With a society living on credit, a government deep in debt, eight years of desensitization during training (something unique to doctors), rising tuition, and falling pay—it's no wonder doctors are having a major problem with debt. Where will it end? Debt has become the norm. Will Rogers summed up this pattern of high consumption on borrowed money nicely.

Too many people spend money they haven't earned to buy things they don't want, to impress people they don't like.

– Will Rogers

Most doctors have seen a long-term diabetic patient sometime during their career. After many years of out-of-control blood sugar, nerve damage begins to take place. The patient begins to lose feeling in his or her feet.

Tim was one such patient with diabetic neuropathy, who bought a new pair of shoes for a vacation to Russia. He walked all over Saint Petersburg in those new tennis shoes. He came home and noted a fever and a bad smell coming from his foot.

Those new shoes had caused a blister on his foot, but he couldn't feel it due to the neuropathy. As he continued to walk on the blister, the damage got worse. Later, the blister popped and the wound became infected. The entire bottom of his foot was lost.

Informing Tim of the need for a below-knee amputation was not easy. He would have none of that. No one was going to cut off his foot. He had been a diabetic for many years and took excellent care of his feet, despite the neuropathy, and he wasn't going to lose one now. He couldn't feel the problem and he couldn't see the problem, but the problem was there nonetheless. The top of his foot, which was all he could see, seemed a little red. I got a mirror so Tim could see the bottom of his foot. Only after personally seeing all the skin and subcutaneous tissue missing, and the tendons and bones visible, did he finally realize there was a problem—a serious problem.

This situation is similar to what debt is doing to doctors in medical school. We don't see the problem, we don't feel the problem, and so what's the big deal? Everyone else is doing it. Doctors are suffering from *debt*abetic neuropathy:

Debt is like poorly fitting shoes on numb feet. Your financial future is rotting away and you're not even aware it's happening.

Eventually the smell gets your attention, but by then it's too late. A bankruptcy (amputation), divorce, or even a suicide may be looming on the horizon.

Don't let debtabetic neuropathy get a foothold on you.

LIFE BEFORE DEBT

Many people never get the opportunity to enjoy their grandparents. Your grandparents may have died when you were too young to know them, lived too far away, or were so frail they couldn't play with you. I was fortunate to have all four of my grandparents and a great-grandmother, not only living within five miles, but also vigorous, active, and eager to play.

I lost both grandfathers to cancer before I was old enough to drive and since I was close to them, it was a heartfelt loss. When I started this book, both my grandmothers were with me still, and I visited them frequently. I have many great memories of my grandparents. Before I finished this book, my oldest grandmother passed away at age 96.

In 2013, things changed when one of my grandmothers, who was diagnosed with Alzheimer's disease a year earlier, took a turn for the worse. During a Christmas visit, for the first time in my life, Grandma didn't know me. I was devastated. Afterwards, I sat in the car holding my wife's hand as the tears rolled down my cheeks. I had lost my grandmother. Her body was there but her mind was not.

With every visit, it became harder for me to remember what she was like before Alzheimer's. Visits to her at the memory care facility have replaced my memories of Grandma. The old memories of my real grandmother have faded.

Many doctors are going through this same phenomenon, only the setting is different. You have spent so much of your life in debt, you can't remember what it was like to be debt-free. You are in the later stages of Alzheimer's *debt*mentia.

You might have borrowed some money for little things while still in high school, but you likely didn't have any debt back then. Living with your parents, a part-time, minimum-wage job was sufficient to provide you with spending money. In general, if you didn't have money in your pocket, you couldn't buy anything. You didn't have a credit card to pull out when you wanted something. You couldn't go to the bank and ask for a home equity loan. You had to save your money before you could spend it.

My first *big kid* bicycle was an orange Schwinn Varsity ten-speed. It was the first *big ticket* item I remember wanting to buy. My parents had agreed to pay for one-third of the cost, if

I provided the rest. It was $112 dollars and I worked hard at odd jobs all summer to save the money. In 1973 there weren't a lot of job opportunities for an eleven-year-old who wanted to buy a bike. By the end of the summer, it was mission accomplished and the bike was mine. I'll never forget the feeling of accomplishment.

Most people can recall a similar childhood experience. It felt so good to bring home the long-sought-after item, when you worked so hard to earn the money first. There was pride of ownership. You seemed to take better care of the things you had to work hard to get. Then somewhere along the way, you forgot that valuable lesson.

The real debt lifestyle began in college. Student loans, car loans, home loans, financed vacations, credit card charges, etc. You changed to a new lifestyle, borrowing to get what you wanted, and forgot the old way of only spending what you had in your pocket. Out with the old and in with the new. You grew so accustomed to debt that it became the natural order.

THE PERPETUAL-DEBT LIFESTYLE

These days when shopping for a car, it seems natural not to look at the total price, but at the monthly payment. It's not about affording the car, but affording the car payment. When I was a second-year resident, my car began visiting the shop too often. Maybe it had a thing for the mechanic. It was a fourteen-year-old Oldsmobile Delta 88 my parents had given me. My wife had nicknamed this very large car *The Boat*. As a resident working 80-110 hours a week, there was no time for the frequent visits to the shop. It was time to replace my car.

As I embarked on the search for a car, I figured my paycheck could handle the payment. I had fallen into the trap of thinking car payment instead of car price. I had forgotten the lesson I learned when saving for my bike. What kind of car was befitting a young new doctor? After all, I would still be driving it at the end of my residency and wanted to look good as a new staff doctor.

Mercedes was the first idea to pop into my head. I'm not sure why, since I didn't know anyone who had one and had never been inside one. It seemed like the right fit for a young doctor's image. With the target car chosen, it was time to proceed to the dealership for a test drive.

In 1990, the Mercedes 300E was priced around $30,000. A seven-year loan would only be about $400 a month. Pulling onto the car lot driving *The Boat* did turn a few heads. What was a guy driving a car like that doing at a Mercedes dealership? When they discovered I was a doctor, they jumped to attention. Their *whale* had arrived.

The test drive was awesome. The look, feel, and smell, and the confidence I experienced while driving down the road were new to me. The sound when the door closed, a good solid *clunk*, was very different from the clink and rattle made when shutting the door on *The Boat*. What a car. Now I knew what the big deal was about owning a Mercedes, and I wanted one. The new car bug had bitten and its venom flowed through my veins. I reluctantly returned the keys and sat down with the salesperson to come up with a deal.

Reality began to set in as I pondered all the things I could do with $30,000 besides driving around in a *very* nice car. Was a car really worth so much money? More than one year's salary? Was more than an entire year of every-other-night call worth a trade for one metal car? How would the $400 payment really affect our spending plan?

My wife and I agreed at the time of our wedding, four months into my internship, to live on only one of our incomes and save the other. We figured if something happened to one of our incomes, it wouldn't hurt us financially since we could live on only one income anyway. Taking on this car payment would mean encroaching on our second income, for the budget to balance.

The salesperson was not pleased to hear me say I would think about it and get back to him. Carolyn and I talked about it over the next few days. We knew it was more than we should spend at that time in our lives.

We had been married more than a year and were establishing a solid financial footing, so I thought I could afford the car. By conventional standards, we could afford the payments. Since it was my dream car, my wife said she would go along with it if I really wanted to buy the car.

The Mercedes never ended up in our garage. After much lamenting, a one-year-old Ford Taurus sat in the driveway. Similar car, but not similar quality. At one-third the price, our spending plan had a lot more breathing room. Regrets never surfaced from the decision to forgo the Mercedes. We have purchased cars since then costing more than the $30,000 sticker price we passed on that day, but we waited until we could pay cash. The easy monthly payments didn't get their hooks into me, so I dodged a bullet. The memory of the Schwinn Varsity came back just in time to save me. It was a lucent moment in my journey with Alzheimer's debtmentia.

About that same time, one of the other residents in my program came driving into the parking lot in a brand new sports car. This guy had been constantly complaining about how depressed his enormous school loan debt made him feel. He was so weighted down, he wondered if he could ever get out from under his debt. When he drove in with a gorgeous new car, I asked him if he won the lottery or inherited some money. How could he afford such a car with all his debt? He said he was getting so depressed he needed a *pick-me-up*, so he bought a new car.

I had a hard time grasping his concept. How could adding more debt and more monthly payments decrease the depression he felt from being in debt? I'm sure he felt better for about a month, until his first car payment was due. Then his depression returned and was probably worse than before.

Like the situation with my grandmother, forgetting what it was like to play with her at home, it's easy to forget what it was like to be debt-free and own everything. Many doctors are suffering from Alzheimer's debtmentia. You have fallen into the *new normal* lifestyle of debt and easy monthly payments. Once you begin, you tend to never go back. It's too easy to have it now and agree to the easy monthly payments, while disregarding the total cost and the effect it will have on your future. Everyone else does it that way. The government does it that way. The neighbor does it that way. Family members do it that way. So why shouldn't you do it that way too? You just don't remember any other way.

There is more to life than increasing its speed.

– Gandhi

SOME DEBT IS HARD TO AVOID

Even if you are doing your best to avoid debt, you may still find yourself in a position where assuming debt is the best available option. How long you carry it, and how you handle it, is up to you.

There are currently few options for students to become doctors without incurring substantial debt. Annual tuition for some schools has exceeded $50,000. Likewise, it is unlikely you will be able to buy your first house without a mortgage.

Many doctors with a large debt burden have fallen prey to the idea of paying their debt off over a long period of time under the false assumption this provides more available spending capacity. The norm seems to be borrow all you can and pay it off over the longest possible term.

This is costing you a lot of money, in the form of interest and a lot of added stress. The longer you delay paying off debts, the more of your wealth is sucked into the interest "black hole." The key to handling debt is to pay it off as fast as possible, while remaining in balance with the present and the future.

IF YOU PAY INTEREST ON IT, IT'S DEBT

Let us look closely at the house-buying process and what a mortgage truly costs. You've probably heard about how great an investment it is to buy a house. Those in housing booms made a profit on their houses, but what happened to those caught up in the housing bust? Buying a house isn't always a moneymaking transaction.

It's easy to forget to factor in the costs of owning the house. Calculating the profit you make on your house usually only involves the original purchase price and the current selling price. Real estate broker fees, maintenance costs, yard care, insurance, taxes, points, loan origination fees—and most of all, the amount of interest you paid on the mortgage—are not usually considered. In fact, when people tell me they are debt-free and I ask when they made their final house payment, they say, "I still have a mortgage. I meant I'm debt-free except for the house." Mortgages are not considered debt to many people. They are considered a normal piece in the puzzle of life.

If you pull up a sample spending plan from any software program, you will never find your house listed in the section titled savings/investments. Your house is usually the first item in the expense section of the plan. Why? Because it's usually the single biggest expense you have. You should never think of your house as an investment. It is an expense, and a big one at that.

Housing purchases tend to be very emotional decisions, and your dreams will often exceed your spending plan. The decision on how much money to spend on a house and how long a period to finance it is likely the most expensive decision you will ever make.

Too much house payment in the spending plan will financially cripple you for decades.

Nothing hits home more than crunching the numbers. Einstein is reported to have said that the most powerful force he knew of on earth was compound interest. Compound interest is the reason some of the biggest buildings in the city are banks. Where do they make all their money? Their source of income is you and me, the ones who borrow money and pay interest. If they can make a lot of money by charging us interest, then we can save a lot of money by avoiding paying that same interest.

Interestingly, this is not a new phenomenon. A few thousand years ago, Solomon stated:

Just as the rich rule over the poor, so the borrower is servant to the lender.

- Proverbs 22:7

What a powerful statement. If you borrow money from some-one, you become their servant/slave. Test it out—try skipping a few mortgage payments and see what happens. The true owners will show up and take possession of their house. Until the final payment is made, the house belongs to the lender. You only thought you were the homeowner, when you were paying all those bills for repairs, insurance, and property taxes. The bank owns the house and you own the expenses. What a deal.

Let's take a closer look at how a mortgage specifically affects doctors. Following conventional wisdom, you would stretch your budget to the max and buy the most expensive house the bank will authorize, make the smallest down payment possible, and stretch out the mortgage for the longest offered period. You then refinance every time the interest rate drops or your house increases in value to *harvest equity*. This plan generates maximum profit for the bank, which of course comes out of your pocket. Let's examine this wisdom closely.

DR. BRITNEY MOREHOUSE

Dr. Britney Morehouse is a private practice physician who purchased a house with a $600,000, 30-year mortgage. Since 1971, house mortgage interest rates have been as high as 18%, and as low as 3%. Most of the time, mortgage rates run in the 6%–8% range. For our illustration, Dr. Morehouse will have a fixed 5.3% interest rate.

This $600,000 mortgage requires a monthly payment of $3,332 in principal and interest. Dr. Morehouse will be making 360 of these payments for a grand total of $1,199,520. For ease of discussion, let's round it off to $1.2 million. Following this plan, Dr. Morehouse will pay $1.2 million for the $600,000 loan. But wait, there's more.

She will need to pay income taxes on her money before netting the $1.2 million she needs to pay off the loan. Assuming an effective combined tax rate (including federal, state, social security, and other payroll taxes) of 40%, Dr. Morehouse must earn $2 million from her practice to pay the tax ($800,000) to net the $1.2 million to pay off the $600,000 loan. That's getting kind of spendy. I wonder if Dr. Morehouse would agree the house is worth the large sum she has to pay. But wait, there's more.

Dr. Morehouse has overhead costs in her practice. Median practice overhead runs about 56%, but let's round it to 50% for simplicity. She will need the practice to collect $4 million to pay the $2 million overhead to pay the $800,000 in taxes to net the $1.2 million she will need to pay off the $600,000 loan. Still, there's more.

She doesn't collect what she bills. The ratio of billings to collections at my old practice ran about 53%. Let's use 50% for simplicity. She will need to bill $8 million to collect the $4 million to pay the $2 million overhead to pay the $800,000 in taxes to net the $1.2 million she will need to pay off the $600,000 loan.

Dr. Morehouse will need to generate $8 million in billings to pay off her $600,000 mortgage. No wonder she is feeling burned out! With numbers like that, it's hard to feel good about taking a vacation or even a day off. This process repeats itself every time she buys something with borrowed money. Second home, motorhome, cars, timeshares, vacations, weddings . . . So much for easy monthly payments.

In the last few months, I have met two surgeons in their 50s who recently refinanced a 30-year mortgage for more than $800,000. They have committed to paying a $4,000 monthly house payment well into their 80s, but they don't intend to work into their 80s. They have both expressed concern they will not have enough money to retire.

How will they make the payment after they retire? Covering the house payment out of their retirement plan will require an additional $2 million in savings. ($2,000,000 x 4% draw = $6,667 a month. After 40% tax, you have $4,000—although taxes might be lower in retirement, so they could get by with less savings). I see why they are worried. One of them sent his family on a vacation, but he stayed home to work, fearing the loss of income. When the cost of your house infringes on other aspects of your life, you are house poor.

Some doctors are planning to sell their big house when they retire, and move to a smaller, less expensive house and put the equity in the bank. If this is your plan, why not downsize now and save a fortune? If you will be doing it anyway, the longer you wait, the more interest you will pay—costing you future wealth. If it is the appreciation you are waiting for, the new, smaller house will continue to appreciate as well.

ANOTHER WAY TO HANDLE MORTGAGE DEBT

There is a better way to handle mortgage debt than convention- al wisdom offers. How would this play out, if Dr. Morehouse paid off the house in seven years instead of 30? Before dismiss- ing this idea—like I did the first time I heard it—let's keep an open mind to the possibility, because it is doable. I did it and so have many others.

To pay this mortgage off in seven years, Dr. Morehouse would need to add $5,234 to each monthly payment, bringing it to $8,566. At the end of seven years, Dr. Morehouse would have made $719,544 in total payments. Let's round that off to $720,000 for simplicity. Contrast that with the 30-year option of $1.2 million. What could she do with that extra $480,000? Take a look at the table that follows for all the numbers.

She will need to bill $4.8 million to collect the $2.4 million to pay the $1.2 million overhead and the $480,000 in taxes to net the $720,000 she will need to pay off the $600,000 loan.

In other words, if Dr. Morehouse chooses to pay her mortgage over 30 years instead of seven years, she would need to generate an extra $3.2 million in billings, or $1.6 million in additional collections—provided she stuck to the 30-year plan and didn't do any refinancing or harvesting of equity.

How would all this relate to Dr. Morehouse's workload? As I am writing this chapter, a mid-level existing patient visit pays me $71.12 if the patient has Medicare and $115.00 if they have Blue Cross. If we were to assume Dr. Morehouse's practice is 50% Medicare and 50% Blue Cross, she would be collecting an average of $93.06 per patient visit. That works out to an extra 17,193 patient visits to collect the $1.6 million she would need to pay the extra interest, if she stretched out the home mortgage to 30 years.

$600,000 MORTGAGE AT 5.3% INTEREST

Loan Expenses	30 Years	7 Years	Difference
Monthly payment	$ 3,332	$ 8,566	$ 5,234
Total principal	600,000	600,000	0
Total interest	600,000	120,000	(480,000)
Total Cost	$ 1,200,000	$ 720,000	(480,000)

Production Needs			
Billings	$ 8,000,000	$ 4,800,000	$ (3,200,000)
Collections (50% of billings)	4,000,000	2,400,000	(1,600,000)
Overhead (50% of collections)	2,000,000	1,200,000	(800,000)
Gross income on W2	2,000,000	1,200,000	(800,000)
Income tax (40% of W2)	800,000	480,000	(320,000)
Net Income Needed for Loan	$ 1,200,000	$ 720,000	$ (480,000)

Work Load Equivalent			
Total collections	$ 4,000,000	$ 2,400,000	$ (1,600,000)
Average collection per patient	$ 93.06	$ 93.06	$ 93.06
Required number of patient visits	42,983	25,790	**(17,193)**

If Dr. Morehouse didn't need to see those extra 17,193 patients, what could she do instead? Take Mondays off? Figuring
35 patients per day and 47 working weeks per year, this would
equate to more than ten years of every Monday off. Maybe she
could stop seeing a particular diagnosis she doesn't like? Could
she come home earlier each day to have dinner with her family?
Make it to all her kids' sporting events and school activities?
Coach her kids' soccer team?

My reward for becoming debt-free was to give up vascular and
thoracic surgery. They represented two areas of my practice I
didn't enjoy, but was afraid to give up. Those were my highest-
reimbursing cases. If I gave them up, I presumed I would lose
significant income and might not be able to meet my expenses.
I was doing something I didn't like, only for the money. That
sounds like a formula for burnout if I ever heard one.

When I became debt-free, I finally had the courage to drop
those cases from my schedule and give them to my partner,
who loved vascular surgery. Interestingly, my income didn't
drop. Those holes in my schedule were filled with other patients who had diagnoses I enjoyed treating. It was a win-win
deal. I got rid of something I didn't like; my partner got more
of what he did like. My income didn't change. I only found
the courage to make that move after I was no longer at risk of
losing my house due to a drop in income. Becoming debt-free
created more options for me, and lowered my stress level.

What could your reward be? One physician I know got rid of disability exams when his debt burden was reduced.

Not all doctors chose to be in private practice like Dr. Morehouse. If you are employed, use the gross income line of the chart for comparison, since your overhead and billing numbers are not usually easy for you to access. But remember, if an employed physician doesn't keep billings high, the employer is going to reconsider the offered gross income.

How will the 17,193 patient visits be affected by a change in reimbursements? Do you think reimbursements will be higher or lower, in the future? I believe reimbursements will be dropping and that would make this scenario even worse.

Another alternative is the 15-year mortgage. Usually it is offered at a lower interest rate than the 30-year mortgage. The combination of fewer years of interest and a lower interest rate often leads to paying only one-third the interest you would have paid on a 30-year mortgage. Getting the lower interest of the 15-year mortgage and paying it off ahead of schedule is even better.

STUDENT LOANS: A MORTGAGE WITHOUT A HOME

The title pretty much sums up the situation with student loans. You finish your training with enough debt to buy a house, but you are homeless. The rest of this chapter is for those of you who are still young, such as residents, students, and young attendings. If you don't have student loans, you can skip this section and start the next chapter.

What's a student to do? If you want to become a doctor and you don't join the military or have wealthy parents, you may have to bite the bullet and pay the price of accumulating a large debt. This is one of the few good uses of debt, since borrowing money to get an education that substantially boosts your income is a good investment.

When you started borrowing money for school, you promised you would pay it off as an attending. At the beginning of your career, don't increase your lifestyle to spend all your new income right away—if ever. Since you have been getting by on $50,000 a year, why not increase your spending just a little, to say $75,000 a year, and use the rest to get rid of your student loans as fast as possible? It's entirely possible for most doctors to pay off those loans in three years—saving tens of thousands of dollars in interest, not to mention the stress relief.

Some doctors may end up in lower-paying positions, and a huge debt burden will sting quite a bit—but there will still be enough money, and it will work out. It may take a little longer, but the same principles apply.

LOAN FORGIVENESS PROGRAMS

The US government offers the Public Service Loan Forgiveness (PSLF) program. In this program, after you work in an approved program for ten years—and often your residency will count towards this—the remaining outstanding loans are forgiven.

If you are considering this plan, you should begin repaying your loans on an income-based repayment plan (IBR) immediately after graduation. They must be government loans in your name. The longer your residency, the more you will benefit from this plan. The key is to make low monthly payments, for as long as possible under the IBR, to get the maximum loan forgiveness. Once you become an attending and your income goes up, your monthly payments go up to a nonsubsidized value, and you will have less deferment and less to be forgiven. If you are reading this as an attending and thinking of beginning this program, you have probably missed this boat, as you are likely making full payments now and won't be able to defer enough interest to reap the benefits.

A long residency allows you to take advantage of several years of reduced payments under IBR—such as five years of general surgery, one year of surgical critical care, and two years of cardiothoracic surgery. You will then have only two years of payments at a higher physician's salary to make before the remainder is forgiven. After eight years of reduced payments on a resident's salary, your benefit will be very large. On the other hand, a three-year family medicine residency will require seven more years of essentially full payments, so the reward will not be as large.

This program has risks you should understand and evaluate. Ten years is a long time to postpone your payments and accumulate interest. A lot can happen in ten years.

If at any time you decide to leave this qualified program, you lose in this deal. If Congress decides to cut the PSLF program out of the budget, you lose. If you choose to work in a place you don't like just to get into this program, you lose. If your place of employment drops off the list of qualified locations, you lose. Only if everything lines up just right do you win.

In order for this to work out optimally, you can't consolidate your loans for lower interest, and you must make the smallest monthly payment possible, for as much of the ten years as possible. This plan accumulates the highest possible interest bill before the government will repay the balance. I believe this is not a risk worth taking.

When you borrowed the money, you did so with the notion you would pay it off when you finished training. The deal was they loan you money, you get a great education so you can earn a lot more money, and then when you are earning the high salary from that education, you pay back the loan. Well, now is when you fulfill that obligation.

NEGOTIATE STUDENT LOAN REPAYMENT INTO YOUR CONTRACT

With today's doctor shortage, it's usually easy to negotiate some loan repayment language into your employment contract.

Many employers are offering this to make their job more attractive to you than another one you might be considering. Asking for it may produce results; not asking for it may leave a lot of money on the table.

Often you will receive a forgivable loan. These can work out well and are designed to incentivize you to stay with them for an extended period. If you leave early, you will need to pay back part of the forgivable loan. That loan may *not* be very forgiving, especially if you used the money for something other than paying down your student loans. In that case, your forgivable loan may put you further into debt. Don't forget about the tax burden of the forgiven part of the loan—that is still yours to pay.

LOAN CONSOLIDATION

I feel the overall best option is to pay off the loan as rapidly as possible, just as I illustrated with the home mortgage earlier. The deleterious effects of interest compounding against you cannot be overemphasized. In addition to paying off the loan ahead of schedule, you can decrease the total amount of interest you pay even more by doing a loan consolidation. As a high-income earner, you are in a lower risk population for student loan debt. Several companies now offer loan consolidation deals. Do an Internet search for *medical school loan consolidation* to find a current list.

Combining loan consolidation and rapid payback, while keeping your spending and saving in good balance, is your best bet.

Chapter 4

HOW TO RECOGNIZE BAD ADVICE

Many financial advisors will discourage you from paying off your home mortgage early. They have many *reasons* for maximizing your portfolio and their profit with money you could have used to pay off debt. Let's cover the two most common ones.

IT'S YOUR LAST GREAT TAX WRITE-OFF

If you hit a patient's patellar tendon with a rubber hammer, the patellar reflex causes their leg to kick out. If you mention paying off your mortgage early, the tax write-off justification will automatically be mentioned. It's the reflex answer.

Never forget the only way to write anything off your taxes is to lose the money (i.e., pay it to the bank in interest). The rewards for your losses are less than you have been led to believe.

To use Dr. Morehouse's situation as an example: Let's assume she is married and filing jointly, so her 2016 standard deduction is $12,600. That means the first $12,600 of her Schedule A deductions don't even count. Everyone gets the standard deduction, even if they have nothing to deduct. Only the portion greater than the standard deduction creates a financial benefit. Also, if Dr. Morehouse is very productive and earns more than $309,900, her itemized deductions will be limited even more. The better you do financially, the less write-off you are allowed. If that's your last great tax write-off, I hate to think about the lesser ones.

Looking at Dr. Morehouse's $600,000 mortgage, the first year's interest will be $31,800. If she has no other deductions to take and doesn't make more than $309,900, then subtracting the standard deduction leaves an effective $19,200 write-off ($31,800 - $12,600). Assuming she pays a 40% combined state and federal tax rate, the $19,200 write-off will save $7,680 in taxes, or 24% of the $31,800 she paid in interest to the bank. For every $100 paid to the bank in interest, the government will give Dr. Morehouse back $24. Even if she could get the full amount of interest as a deduction, it would only generate $40 in refund for every $100 deducted (lost). If you think that is a great deal, then feel free to send me the $100 instead of giving it to the bank and I'll be happy to return $80! That would be twice as good as the write-off.

Dr. Morehouse is better off keeping the $100 and paying the government $40 in taxes. She will have $60 in her pocket instead of $24. *She is out more money by paying interest than by paying taxes.* For every $100 she earns that's spent on interest, she will keep $24 after the deduction. The same $100 kept in her pocket will cost her $40 in taxes, leaving $60 available to spend. So what would Dr. Morehouse prefer to keep for her hard-earned $100: $60 or $24? Dr. Morehouse should pay the mortgage off early and keep the money. She earned it!

INTEREST DEDUCTION

Action	Paying interest	Debt-free
Earned income	$ 100	$ 100
Pay interest to bank	(100)	0
Taxes refunded, 24%	24	0
Taxes paid, 40%	0	(40)
Spendable Cash	$ 24	$ 60

KEEPING THE LOW-INTEREST MORTGAGE AND INVESTING FOR A HIGHER RETURN

This is the second reason most commonly used for not paying off the mortgage early. If everything goes perfectly according to plan:

✓ you don't spend any of the money you were supposed to invest,

✓ your investments get a higher return than the mortgage interest rate you are paying,

✓ you don't lose your job while you still have a mortgage,

✓ *and* the planets all align . . .

When all of the above work out, you could make a little bit of money off the interest difference between the mortgage and the investments. So this one has a smidgen of truth to it, but it's far from a sure thing and very risky.

Why not go for the sure thing and the peace of mind? I have never encountered anyone who was sorry they paid off their home mortgage early. If someone were to pay off their mortgage early and become the first person to ever regret it, then they could always refinance the house and be back where they started.

I know one family who paid off their mortgage and then, a few years later, they took out a new mortgage to do some home improvements and buy an RV. It didn't take long before they regretted going back into debt. They didn't repeat that mistake when they paid off the mortgage early the second time.

I've seen several physicians go through a tough time at the office and, through no fault of their own, had a drop in income. During this time, they were unable to make the mortgage payments and lost their houses. This would not have been the outcome if they had paid off the mortgage and actually owned their houses when their income fell.

Would anyone consider taking out a second mortgage on their house, adding to the risk of foreclosure, in order to invest the money in the stock market? For most of us the answer is no. When put like that it even sounds silly.

If we keep the low-interest loan and invest for a higher return, we are effectively doing just that. We're borrowing against the house and putting it at risk to buy stocks. I have heard this referred to as the *Low-Interest Dilemma*. I don't see a dilemma. Pay off the house—don't use it as a piggy bank. It is your home, not an investment or leverage. Your personal house never shows up in the investment section of a budget, always in the expense section. Your goal is to minimize expenses.

Smoking five cigarettes is not as bad as smoking twenty. Likewise, paying 4% interest is not as bad as paying 10%. But make no mistake, the 4% interest and the five cigarettes are both still bad—but not as bad as the higher alternative. Lowering the interest rate does not make paying interest good, but it will cost less. Anytime compound interest is working against you, it's bad. Anytime compound interest is working for you, it's good. If it's working against you, the lower the interest, the better. Strive for the best though, which is zero interest.

This reminds me of the story of a police officer who ticketed a man for rolling through a stop sign. The man explained to the officer how he had slowed way down and that was effectively the same as stopping. It was close enough. The officer began to hit the man on the thigh with his baton. The man yelled for the officer to stop. The officer asked if he should stop, or slow down, since they were effectively the same. The message got through. We need to stop paying interest, not slow down or reduce the interest. Lower interest is better, but not the best.

People who use this strategy of investing rather than paying off their mortgage tend to continue this pattern indefinitely. Every few years, they refinance for a better rate, to purchase a bigger house or to harvest equity. Their mortgage tends to grow with time. Eventually they find themselves ready to retire with a larger mortgage than when they started. They never make headway, and are paying interest and risking their home for their entire life.

The interest slowly eating away your wealth is like that seemingly innocuous drive-through drink you buy every day. You think it is only 500 calories, so it's no big deal. Five hundred calories, seven days a week, is 3,500 calories—which equates to one pound of fat. After a year, that little drink will add 52 pounds to your waistline and lighten your wallet by $1,600.

Paying off the mortgage also creates more cash flow in the current spending plan. If Dr. Morehouse did not have a mortgage, she would have an extra $3,332 available to spend each month. If her budget becomes tight, this could make a big difference.

One client of mine, I'll call him Dr. Green, was following the principle of investing instead of paying off his low-interest mortgage. He came to me to discuss his pending retirement. He planned to retire after five more years of investing and wanted my confirmation he was on track. After looking over his financial position, I suggested he take some of his savings and pay off his mortgage. If he didn't have the mortgage to pay, he already had enough money saved to cover his other expenses in retirement. He was planning to work five more years to have enough saved in his retirement account to retire with a mortgage. Eliminating the payment eliminated the need for more savings. He went home and talked it over with his wife, then paid off the house and retired one month later. Sometimes the answer is right in front of you, but you can't see it.

As time goes by, the balance owed on your mortgage drops and the payoff amount becomes smaller, but the monthly payment stays the same. The older the mortgage, the better your percentage return in cash flow is if you pay it off.

If Dr. Morehouse were down to her last $100,000 of principal on her mortgage, she would eliminate a $3,332 monthly payment with her $100,000 mortgage payoff. That $3,332 would be money in her pocket, each month, or almost $40,000-a-year guaranteed cash flow. Where else could she put $100,000 and generate a guaranteed $40,000 cash in hand the first year? If she made 8% on an investment, the $100,000 would generate

$8,000 before taxes. Most doctors would prefer their spending plan had the extra $40,000 to utilize, especially if they are nearing retirement.

When you choose to gamble in the stock market for a higher return than the interest you are paying on your home mortgage, you are presuming on the future. It sounds good on paper, but it's not a sure thing. Your returns can be lower than expected. You could lose your income and then lose your home. If you don't have a mortgage, your house won't be at risk if your income falls.

Everything always looks good on paper. New ventures never go out of business on paper, yet 80% fail. No one goes bankrupt on paper, yet it happens all the time. No one loses their job on paper, yet I have seen physicians fired at a moment's notice. Many physicians have lost their homes because they couldn't keep up with the payments. Don't become one of the statistics.

When you pay off your house, you are getting a sure thing. When you invest in the market, you are taking a chance and betting you will make money; often you do, but not always. It's a risk you don't need to take. You will sleep better knowing your home is secure and the title is yours.

People use many other reasons/excuses for keeping the mortgage and stretching it out as long as possible, but they don't usually consider the total cost spread out over a lifetime. You will only generate a finite amount of earnings in your lifetime. Strive to give up as little as possible to the bank in the form of interest, thus keeping the maximum for your lifetime personal use and investing. Borrowing money to play with today means there will be even less to play with tomorrow.

CONFLICTS OF INTEREST

Often the people who are advising you to stretch out the mortgage have a conflict of interest when giving the advice. The advisor who makes money on your investment decisions is like the pharmaceutical rep who is telling you all about his new medication and why it is better than what you already use. The advice might be fine, but due to the obvious bias/conflict of interest, you never know when information is tipped in their favor. When you read a study about a new wonder drug and notice the manufacturer financed it, you tend to take the information with a grain of salt. Use the same skepticism with your financial advisors. Follow the money. Many a doctor has dropped his financial advisor after discovering the advisor was making more money off the portfolio than the doctor was.

Let's take a look at who is offering this advice.

The banker: If the bank holds your mortgage, they will continue to make a profit as long as you keep the mortgage and continue to pay interest. If the bank sells their mortgages, they make money by writing new loans (points, loan origination fee, and setup fees), so they would profit if you refinance and harvest some equity. If a competing bank holds the mortgage, then any money sent to the other bank to pay off that mortgage will not be available for you to deposit in a savings account or certificate of deposit in their bank, which your banker could loan out to make even more money. He is biased and has no reason to encourage you to pay off your house. He makes no profit if you pay off your house.

Stockbroker: A commissioned broker only makes money when you buy and sell stock. The more he can convince you to churn your account, the more money he makes. If you use your available cash to pay off a mortgage, that money will not be available to buy more stock and pay his fees. He is biased and has no reason to encourage you to pay off your house.

Insurance salesperson: Many of the insurance products they peddle are great for the insurance company and the salesperson's commission but are bad for you, the buyer. This is true for any kind of life insurance that is also an investment. Commissions come directly out of your pocket and are not available for the investment. Like the other listed advisors, if you use your available cash to pay off the mortgage, it will not be available to buy the overpriced, high-commission policy he wants to sell. (Only buy term life insurance and never use insurance as an investment.) He is biased and has no reason to encourage you to pay off your house.

Advisor paid on total portfolio: Some advisors are paid a percentage of your total portfolio value. The larger the balance in your investment account, the larger the advisor's paycheck. If you use your money to pay off your house, it is not in your portfolio to raise his income. He is biased and has no reason to encourage you to pay off your house.

Accountant: Many accountants are really tax preparers in disguise. You do need to have a top-notch accountant/CPA, not simply a tax preparer. Tax preparers may not be after what is best for you overall, but rather what creates the most deductions. The more tax deductions they can put on your tax return, the more it looks like they are earning their fee. "See what I did for you." Unfortunately, the things that create the most deductions are not always the best options.

Deductions are good, but only if you had to spend the money anyway. Remember, the reason you can claim a deduction is because you've lost money. As mentioned before, to lose one dollar in interest and gain 24 cents in tax refund is not a good deal by itself. To get the 24-cent refund for something you already had to pay anyway is a better deal. You don't have to pay mortgage interest. If you didn't have anything to deduct, you might not need someone to prepare your taxes. An accountant is less biased than the others, but has no motivation to encourage anyone to pay off their house.

Unbiased advisor: An unbiased advisor will not be selling anything or making any profit based on the decisions you make or the size of your portfolio. This person has your best interests in mind. If you do well, you tell your friends, and he gets more clients. He has no biases to keep him from recommending you pay off your mortgage, if it's in your best interest. This is the financial planner who is paid a fee for his time, not a commission or percentage of anything. This is the advisor you need to find.

Except for the unbiased advisor, the preceding examples are often salespeople masquerading as financial planners. They have their own best interests in mind and if they can help you along the way, that's a bonus. Some are legitimately trying to help you, but only inasmuch as it helps them also.

When I first set up my IRA during my internship, I went to an investment firm. The advisor helped me set up my IRA. The mutual fund he recommended had the highest front-end load allowable by law. In other words, it was the investment option making him the most money. He was only steering me to the investments that were lucrative for him.

I haven't had a home mortgage since October 2001. Compound interest has been working for me and not against me all that time. So how would Dr. Morehouse be affected if she did the same? Conventional Plan A would be to pay off her mortgage over 30 years with no refinancing or harvesting of equity. This would mean she would pay about $1.2 million over the 30 years ($600,000 in interest) and would have no additional savings.

In Plan B, she made extra monthly payments at first, paid off the mortgage over seven years, and then put the regular house payment of $3,331.83 into her retirement plan, which is invested in the stock market at an 8% average return over the next 23 years. She will pay $720,000 in the first seven years ($120,000 in interest) and own her house. Then the extra money she was paying toward the mortgage is put back into her lifestyle. The $3,331.83 a month original mortgage payment, invested for the remaining 23 years, would result in a $2,627,918 balance.

Plan A at 30 years = house paid off and no investments.

Plan B at 30 years = house paid off and $2,627,918 invested.

I'll take plan B where compound interest is turned around to work for me as soon as possible. In fact, that is exactly what I did. The security you feel when you have no mortgage is hard to quantify. The extra days you take off from work without a mortgage are fun to enjoy and hard to quantify.

I hope these numbers help make the case for paying off your mortgage early. You work hard for your money. The bank doesn't deserve to have it more than you do!

Chapter 5

NEW PERSPECTIVES ON DEBT AND HOUSING

OWNING TOO MUCH HOUSE CAN CRIPPLE YOUR FINANCES

It's easy to get caught up in the house-buying frenzy and end up with too much house for your budget, making you house poor. After so many years of depriving yourself during your training, when you finally start making money you feel you deserve a nice house. But at what cost? Does having five acres instead of one really make you happier? Will 5,000–10,000 square feet improve your well-being more than 3,500 square feet? If you bought the house for your family, but then you stay at work late to earn the money to pay for it and never see them, who are you kidding?

If you are overextended with too much house, there won't be enough money left for all the other things you need and would like to have. What will you have to eliminate? The dream car?

New clothes? Vacations? Your retirement savings? Your children's college fund? Make no mistake, the extra money will have to be pulled from something. Is it really worth the trade?

How will it feel when you tell your children you would like to help them with their college costs, but instead you put the money into your expensive house? Did they enjoy the yard more than they would enjoy a college education without debt? Did you? Did your children enjoy going on vacation without one of their parents, who had to stay home working to make the house payment?

When I get ready to take a patient to surgery, I explain the procedure, alternatives, and risks. Only after I'm certain they understand what they are getting into, will I be satisfied if they make a decision to opt out of a needed surgery.

The same goes for your house purchase. Make sure you have counted the costs, checked the procedure, alternatives, and risks, and realized what you will be giving up to have that house. Otherwise, after buying too much house for your budget and struggling financially for the rest of your life, you may look back with regret.

A FEW HOUSE-BUYING TIPS

1. Buy a house only when it fits into the plan. If that means renting while getting on firm financial footing (e.g., not

drowning in debt), that's OK. Expanding your lifestyle slowly will allow you to get all the pieces in place before committing to the house payment. If you commit too soon, before you have accounted for everything in the spending plan—like disability insurance payments, for example—you may find yourself with too little money left to get everything you need. If you buy too soon, you may not be able to pay off your student loans quickly, and will pay unnecessary interest on them for years.

2. Don't buy a house as a resident or new attending. Wait until you know you are in a practice you'll want to stay in for more than five years. Avoid the forced sell at the end of residency, or if you discover you don't like the job you picked. The market might be down and you don't need the extra hassle at that point in your life.

3. Don't take on a home mortgage greater than two and one-half times one spouse's or partner's income. This will leave plenty of space in the spending plan for all the other things life throws at you. It also keeps the two-wage-earning family safe if one of them loses their job. If you are in a higher-paying specialty, use an even lower multiple of your income.

4. Don't buy a house to *keep up with the Dr. Joneses*; buy a house that meets your needs. The Dr. Joneses of the world are going broke—you don't want to be like them. Fully

understand what you need and what you can afford, and let those issues guide you more than what you want and what the bank will loan you.

5. Pay off the mortgage as fast as possible, and then start earning interest instead of paying interest. The quicker you turn interest around and have it work for you instead of against you, the quicker you will reach your financial goals.

6. Never think of your personal residence as an investment. It's an expense. Always work to minimize expenses. If you think of it as an investment, it will taint your decision. You may get a bigger house to make a better investment, and the added accompanying expenses could push you into bankruptcy and foreclosure.

7. Never treat your house like a piggy bank, harvesting equity or taking a second mortgage to buy something. No car, boat, motorcycle, motorhome, or any other toy is worth putting your home at risk. None of those things feels as good as being debt-free.

8. Never get an adjustable-rate mortgage. It's not worth the risk. Many people have lost their houses because of interest rate increases. Most people stretch their budget to the max to buy a house, leaving no room for the adjustable rate to adjust the payments higher. When it happens, you may end up in foreclosure.

9.   If you find your house is too expensive and is choking out your spending plan, sell it. It is not worth the trouble it is causing you. The sooner you make the move, the better. It's only a building; you can find another one. One that fits into your income better and creates much more happiness.

Never let a house become a ball and chain attached to your leg. Make it instead a sanctuary of peace and tranquility.

DEBT IS OFTEN AN UNNECESSARY RISK

Every doctor has experienced *that* patient. The one with so many medical problems and medications you don't understand how he can still be alive. But there he is, sitting on the exam table, seeking your help.

Mine was a 65-year-old white male with alcoholic cirrhosis, ascites, COPD, diabetes, atrial fibrillation, hypertension, and—among other things—congestive heart failure. He had a list of medications longer than my arm, including prednisone for his lungs and Coumadin for his atrial fibrillation. He was in the resident clinic and I was a fourth-year surgery resident, working him up for his painful umbilical hernia. It was large but not incarcerated.

He told me, "Doc, you've got to do something. I don't like having this thing sticking out in front of me. It bugs me."

I finished the examination and presented the case to my attending, who asked what I thought we should do. I said it would be a risky surgery, but he was complaining about it so I thought we should fix the hernia. He leaned back in his chair and said something to me I never forgot:

Don't poke a skunk.

"Even though he might have some symptoms with the hernia, the situation might be made worse if we take him to the operating room. He is likely to have complications and may not even survive the surgery. He has been living with the hernia up until now; he can live with it a bit longer. *Don't poke a skunk.*"

That moment was burned into my memory. I've been in similar situations since and the conversation keeps coming back to me. *Don't poke a skunk.*

If you poke a skunk, you might get away with it and you might not. You might have a great story to tell or you might end up soaking in a tomato juice bath tonight. It's a risk you don't need to take.

Several years ago, my family started riding quads (all-terrain vehicles) in the Oregon sand dunes. One day, we came upon a lake in the dunes. One side of the lake was right up against a cliff of sand about 100 feet tall. People riding along the side of the cliff with their quads could look to the left, down the cliff, and see the water. Looking to the right, up the cliff, is the sky. It looked like a great thrill. My kids wanted to do it. This was a good teaching moment. I told them, *"Don't poke a skunk."*

They didn't get it. So I explained to them, even though it may be a lot of fun and a great adrenaline rush, the consequences of a mistake were high. I said, "If you hit a bump and your thumb touches the kill switch, you and your quad are going swimming. If your quad quits on the side of the hill or runs out of gas, you and the quad are going swimming."

So they commenced to explain to me how those things rarely happened and since it was unlikely to happen, it should be OK. Since it was me who was paying for the quad, it would be no skin off their nose if it went swimming. Dad would fix it. When I told them they would be responsible for the $2,000 it would take to repair the quad after a swimming trip, there was a lot less interest in riding the side of that hill.

The likelihood of a bad outcome should not drive our decision. The consequences should prevail.

Yes, falling in the lake had low odds, but if it did happen, it would be very expensive. And it did happen: every month we saw someone who had fallen into the lake being towed back to the campground. *Don't poke a skunk.* It's a risk you don't need to take.

Acquiring and maintaining debt is also a risk you don't need to take. Most of the time, you can get away with it. You have been getting away with it for many years, as you borrowed your way through medical school. You may get away with it, if you buy a house that stretches your spending plan or a car you really can't afford. Then one day, when you're not paying close enough attention, or something you hadn't planned on occurs, you will find yourself in a financial mess that wouldn't exist had you avoided the debt in the first place. *Don't poke a skunk.* It's a risk you don't need to take.

When you borrow money, you are presuming on tomorrow.

Whenever you borrow money, you have committed to using some of next year's income to pay for this year's indulgence. What if next year doesn't go as planned? What if your finger happens to touch the kill switch? What if pregnancy comes around a little sooner than planned and morning sickness makes it impossible to work? What if a fall on a hiking trip fractures a few bones, and results in a six-month disability? What if Congress passes a new law that makes it unprofitable for hospitals to employ doctors? No one ever knows when a stroke is coming, as it did for one of my internal medicine friends. His career came to a sudden and unexpected end.

The future holds many uncertain and unknown events. When you borrow money, you are assuming your circumstances will continue unchanged, and you will be able to pay off your loan with future earnings. Isn't that why you borrowed money in medical school? You assumed your income would be greater as an attending and you could pay all the money back then. What if your career path changes? What if your dream changes from joining a private practice to becoming a village doctor at a medical mission hospital in a third world country? With all that debt to pay, such an option may be off the table. What if a parent has a stroke and they need you close by for help, but they live in a depressed small town where doctors aren't paid so well? What if your parents need to move into assisted living on your dime? What if your sister and her husband die in an accident and you are suddenly raising two more children? If you have too much debt, you may limit your options or face financial hardship.

On the other hand, what if you were debt-free when any of these events occurred? You can be open to making all kinds of moves if you don't have any debt.

Debt takes away some of your freedom.

Debt takes away some of your future income.

Debt takes away some of your options.

Debt can severely limit your lifestyle choices.

I know several physicians who are feeling burned out. They need to back away from their practice and take some time off to pull themselves together. They need some recuperation time and maybe even a sabbatical—but debt is making it impossible to decrease their work hours. Options are lost. They poked the skunk and the skunk won.

During the housing market crash in the late 2000s, many people declared bankruptcy or gave their houses back to the bank. Why did that happen? Their income usually didn't change. Their mortgage payments didn't change (unless they were foolish enough to fall into the adjustable-rate mortgage trap). Yet they were walking away from their houses.

Many of them refused to pay more money for a house than it was worth. If the mortgage was greater than the house value, they walked away. It ruined their credit rating and their reputation.

The irony of the decision was they already had agreed to pay way more for the house than it was worth, when they agreed to pay interest for 30 years.

One friend in the construction business built multiple houses that he had floated on loans. When the housing crash happened, his business was so upside down he saw no other way out but to take his own life. Presuming upon tomorrow cost him his life. He was borrowing money during the good times, expecting the good times to continue. There will always be both good years and bad years. Your plans need to work for both.

Plan as if next year will be a good year, and you will go bankrupt if you are wrong. Plan as if next year will be a bad year, and you can enjoy it, good or bad.

Bankruptcy and debt go hand in hand. The more debt you carry, the higher the chance something will happen to push you into bankruptcy. You fall into the lake with your quad.

During the 1990s, this country had a great economic boom. Here was a chance to get ahead financially, pay off debt, and stuff a lot of money into retirement accounts. The same chance was available to the government, as everyone paid higher taxes with the increased prosperity. But that's not how it turned out.

During that very prosperous time, many were spending their money as fast as they could make it, and then some. Debt was climbing when debt should have been decreasing. People presumed on tomorrow and borrowed even more. Times were good and getting better, so they assumed they would have even more money next year. Borrowing and spending maxed out. Credit card debt climbed. Mortgage debt climbed. Car debt climbed. They forgot about this time-tested wisdom:

Make hay while the sun shines.

When times are good, resist the temptation to spend and borrow. Good times are the best times to be saving, getting ready to weather future storms. Fill the loft with hay, so you can feed the cows in the winter when the grass is snow-covered. Pay off your debts. Put money into your savings and retirement accounts. Pay off your house. Then when the bad times hit—and they will—you will be ready to weather the storm.

When the housing bubble broke, many people went bankrupt. Contractors were stretched to the max and couldn't sell houses for enough to pay their debts. During a time when we, as a country, should have been in a great economic position, we spent the time sticking our necks out. *Don't poke a skunk.* It's a risk you don't need to take.

Had we shored up our finances in the 90s while prosperity abounded, the crash in the next decade wouldn't have amounted to much. We could have easily weathered the storm, because the hay would have been in the barn when winter set in. As with my cirrhotic hernia patient, there are risks you don't need to take. *Don't poke a skunk.* You might not like the results. Don't make this mistake. When you are doing well, pay off your debt; don't borrow more, expecting to continue to do well forever.

WHAT IF YOU'RE DROWNING IN DEBT?

Some doctors are not merely in debt, they are drowning in debt. They are desperately looking for something to grab ahold of to keep from drowning. At this point, drastic measures are needed. A major change must take place to get back in balance. All efforts need to focus on debt reduction at this point.

I counseled one doctor who had a sudden and permanent drop in income and asked me what he should do. Looking over his spending plan revealed he was falling $5,000 further in the hole every month. A drastic change was needed and fast. I told him the only good option in his plan was to sell his lavish house and get a less expensive one. It was his riverside dream home and he wasn't interested in selling. But there was no other place to cut $5,000 a month. He went away dissatisfied with my advice.

Six months later and another $30,000 in the hole, he put his dream house up for sale.

He had no other solution, yet it took another six months for him to come to grips with it. He sold the house quickly and moved into a less expensive house, and within three months of the decision, he had regained financial balance.

> When you find yourself in a hole, stop digging.
>
> – Will Rogers

When you are in a bad way financially, it will take a big move to correct it. Clipping coupons will not cut it. You may need to sell a house that is crushing you, or that new sports car you can't really afford. You may need to work additional shifts or take extra call to make more money to improve the situation. In general, doctors do not have an income problem—they make good money. They usually suffer from an expense problem and are not willing to face it.

> The biggest problem you will face is simply facing the problem.

I have counseled numerous doctors in financial dire straits, and often found things could easily be solved by changing to a less expensive house. Often that single move made them debt-free and able to restart their financial journey in a balanced and healthy fashion. Breathing room and peace of mind are within their grasp. Once they are out from under the burden of drowning debt, they are able to plot a course for success. Until they can come to grip with the true problem, they can't stop drowning.

Smokers don't quit smoking when you tell them to quit, they quit when *they* decide to quit. You can't get someone else to lose weight until they commit to that goal. Getting out of debt is the same. Until you personally make the decision to do it, it will not happen. However, once the decision is made, it is a simple process to accomplish. Your eyes are now open to the possibilities and you can begin making changes.

If you want something to change, you have to change something.

Make the decision to get your finances back under control, and it will happen. Doctors are smart people, and anyone who can survive medical training can do what it takes to become debt-free.

Chapter 6

FROM DECISION TO DEBT-FREE IN FOUR EASY STEPS

Now that you've decided to become debt-free, the hardest part is over and the fun begins. So let's start at the beginning and get you out of debt as quickly as possible.

STEP ONE: ASSESS THE PROBLEM

When Mr. Thompson comes in to discuss the treatment of his newly diagnosed lung cancer, you don't get out a knife and start cutting before formulating a plan. You gather preliminary information to get an accurate diagnosis and staging. Coordinating a plan for treating a debt problem isn't much different.

You need an accurate analysis of your current financial position. In other words, you need to determine what your current net worth is. For most new doctors, especially right after training, your net worth is negative. Debts exceed assets, and you are in the red. Don't despair if that is the case—you are not alone. That may be the very reason you're reading this book. Whatever your net worth is, use it as the starting point for tracking your progress.

Total up all your assets. Only count real financial assets. Those new golf clubs are quite an asset on the course, and the carbon frame bicycle is an asset to your fitness, but neither is much help in your financial portfolio. Only count cash in the bank, stocks, bonds, mutual funds, investment real estate, retirement plans, health savings accounts, investment art, cash value of insurance, and any other financial assets that are easily convertible to cash, as well as your house value and automobile values. That takes care of the plus side of your net worth calculation.

Next, you need the other side of the equation: a list of all your liabilities or debts. Don't get a piece of scratch paper and list a best guess. You wouldn't do that with Mr. Thompson's cancer, so don't do it here. You would be able to tell Mr. Thompson the tissue type, exact size of the tumor, whether or not the lymph nodes are involved, and the pathological characteristics of the tumor. Use this same attention to detail when totaling your outstanding debts. You need the exact remaining balance, interest rate, monthly payment, and the expected payoff date.

Now take the total of all the assets and subtract the total outstanding debts to get your net worth.

Total Assets - Total Debts = Net Worth

Are the results surprising? Better or worse than expected? Do you have any assets you don't need, that could be sold to improve your position immediately? I know one person who had a stack of gold bars in his safe. There was enough gold to pay off several of his outstanding debts. When he looked at his assets and liabilities on paper, selling the gold to pay off some debt made sense.

Most doctors go through a predictable financial path over the course of their careers. During the learning years, they are borrowing money with almost no assets and begin their careers deep in the red—a negative net worth. Then they graduate and begin to reverse this process as they start the earning years: paying debts and accumulating assets. Most doctors will eventually cross over into the black: a positive net worth. Many years later, they have accumulated enough to retire and live happily ever after while spending their saved money: the burning years. Or so the fairy tale goes.

Every doctor is at a different stage along this continuum. It really doesn't matter where you start, as long as you accurately establish the starting point and begin moving in the right direction, toward the black. Once you are moving, keep track of how your net worth progresses on a quarterly basis. You should see a larger net worth every quarter, or be able to explain what happened to decrease your net worth. The progress will be visible.

STEP TWO: ESTABLISH YOUR GOALS

It is important to establish your goals before making a spending plan. If one of your goals is to be debt-free in five years, then you will put the monthly figures needed to accomplish this goal into your plan. If you establish a plan before making goals, your goals won't be included and your allocations won't likely be in the right places to achieve your desired outcome.

For example, if you have a huge house payment in the spending plan and it eats up your income, you will be tempted to say there is no money left over to reach your goal of being debt-free in five years. If, on the other hand, you put the money into the plan to be debt-free in five years and then you can't balance the spending plan with the large house payment . . . you will realize your house payment is too large to fit into your plans.

If you want to reach your goals, you have to develop a plan to reach them. They will not be accomplished on their own. Do you want to buy a $35,000 new car in two years? Is there a vacation to New Zealand on the horizon? Do you want to retire at age 55? Whatever your financial goals, now is the time to calculate their cost and plan for their accomplishment.

STEP THREE: ESTABLISH A SPENDING PLAN

Most doctors have never used or even seen a spending plan. If that is you, then the first time you do this may be more difficult than you think it should be. However, once a proper plan is established, the power to use it to achieve your financial goals will become evident. Understanding and controlling exactly where the money goes is the key to your financial future.

One day, I was sitting in the lounge with another physician and we got on the subject of budgeting. He rolled his eyes and said, "You expect me to live on Top Ramen and peanut butter?" Thoughts of medical school ran through his mind.

You probably had a similar feeling when I listed this step. If you push out those negative feelings about using a budget or spending plan, it will open you up to total control of your finances. What are *your* negative feelings about making a spending plan?

Medical students say they have too **little** income to need a spending plan.

Residents say they are too **busy** to make a spending plan.

Attending physicians say they have too **much** income to need a spending plan.

Seems it's never a good time to make a spending plan. In reality, it doesn't take a lot of time and the amount of income is not relevant. Living within a spending plan will maximize your financial efficiency at all income levels.

Imagine it as a road map. If you were to set out for Disneyland, you would need a map to get there. If you take off in the car and drive wherever you feel like driving, you are unlikely to arrive at Disneyland. You need a map or a GPS device to tell you when to make the right turns. Likewise, if you spend money whenever and wherever you feel like it, you won't arrive at your chosen financial destination.

The spending plan works the same as a map. It will guide your money use and enable you to arrive at your chosen destination—whether it's a new car, a trip to Paris, paying your children's college tuition, or anything else you might like to achieve financially. Your plan will take you there. If you fly by the seat of your pants, you are unlikely to achieve your goals.

There are many budgeting software systems out there to choose from, including the old-fashioned paper and pencil method. Whatever method you choose, be consistent, accurate, and realistic. You cannot have a spending plan with more money spent than earned each month. Don't be surprised or discouraged if the first draft comes out negative (more spent than earned). It will usually require a few months to hone in on the plan and get it into the black.

There are two specific reasons for a spending plan right now. First, you must assure you are living within your means and aren't risking accumulating more debt. Second, you need to figure out exactly how much money is available each month to put toward paying off debt. This figure is identified by making an accurate plan. After all, it won't do any good to put extra money toward your debt this month, only to find it was needed for a forgotten insurance payment next month.

Over the first few months of use, the forgotten items and the underestimated ones will surface. The plan may look good initially, only to move into the red after these missing items are added. These forgotten items tend to push people over budget. Periodic expenses are often missed in the initial plan: Christmas presents, birthday presents, life insurance payments, haircuts, property taxes, the true amount of those morning drive-through coffee stops. Divide once-a-year items, like life insurance, into twelve payments to come up with a monthly figure to put in the plan.

It's easy to underestimate the cost of small, repetitive items such as coffee. The $5.95 espresso purchased 20 times a month is $119, but you might have only estimated $50 a month when first entering it into the spending plan. Don't guess how much is spent—know where your money goes. Carry a small note pad around and record every item you buy until the plan is complete and accurate.

Prescription for Financial Succe$$
DrCorySFawcett.com · Helping Health Care Professionals Thrive

SPENDING PLAN

A. Benefits Paid by Employer _____
  Retirement plan
  Health insurance
  HSA
  Other (_____)

B. Gross Monthly Income _____
  Salary
  Interest
  Dividends
  Other (_____)

LESS:
1. Tithe (10% of A+B) _____

2. Tax (fed., state, FICA) _____

NET SPENDABLE INCOME _____
  (= Gross-Tithe-Tax)

3. Housing _____
  Mortgage (rent)
  Insurance
  Taxes
  Electricity
  Gas
  Water
  Sanitation
  Telephone
  Internet
  Maintenance
  Other (_____)

4. Food _____

5. Automobile(s) _____
  Payments
  Gas and oil
  Insurance
  License/taxes
  Maint./repair/replace

6. Insurance _____
  Life
  Medical
  Disability
  Other (_____)

7. Clothing _____

8. Debts
  Credit cards
  Student loans
  Other (_____)

9. Recreation
  Eating out
  Activities/trips
  Vacation
  Other (_____)

10. Medical Expenses _____
  Doctor
  Dentist
  Drugs
  Other (_____)

11. School/Childcare _____
  Tuition
  Materials
  Transportation
  Daycare
  Other (_____)

12. Miscellaneous _____
  Toiletry, cosmetics
  Beauty, hair stylist
  Laundry, cleaning
  Allowances, lunches
  Subscriptions
  Gifts (incl. Christmas)
  Cash
  Other (_____)

13. Savings _____

14. Investments _____

TOTAL EXPENSES _____

INCOME VERSUS EXPENSES
  Net Spendable Income _____
  Less Total Expenses – _____
  Discretionary Income _____

First, account for everything your employer pays for your benefit, such as retirement contributions, health insurance premiums, and a health savings account contribution. These numbers will not be used in calculating your available spending money. They should be used when calculating your tithe, if that is a part of your life. The tithe is a tenth portion of your income. The employer's contribution to your retirement plan is your money to spend; just because it didn't show up in your paycheck doesn't mean you shouldn't pay a tithe on it. Account for it in this section and add it to your gross income when figuring your tithe.

Then, account for every income source. If your salary includes a year-end bonus, you may not be able to make an accurate estimate. Don't include bonuses; establish your budgeted income with your known monthly salary. Bonuses and tax refunds are nice to use as extra money but not as part of the spending plan. Since you can't count on them, don't put them in the plan.

Next, consider giving to your church or another charity. Giving is a very freeing experience. You realize how good you have it when you can help others who are less fortunate. I remember a conversation one Christmas when my friend, who was complaining about his financial situation, realized he didn't have it so bad after all. As he made out a check for a Christmas giving basket program, it dawned on him that he was on the giving end of the program, not the receiving end. For the first time, he had a different perspective on his situation. What he perceived as terrible wasn't so bad, taken in the context of other people's situations.

Decide on what a reasonable giving amount would be and take it off the top. If tithing is important, take a tenth of the gross household income and put it into your plan first. Others may argue the tithe should be based on net income, but I think that's the wrong approach. If the government changes the tax rate and your earned income didn't change, why should your tithe change simply because the government changes their rules? When you fill out your tax form and they ask you how much you earned, you don't write down the net, you use the gross. If that is what you earned, that is what you should use to determine your tithe.

Next, take out taxes. Don't fall into the trap, if you are self-employed, of not paying taxes as the money comes in. This can get doctors into deep trouble. When taxes are postponed, often because there are urgent bills to pay, the resulting year-end balance due could be crippling. You never want to find yourself owing the government taxes you don't have money to pay. Keep taxes current.

After removing charitable giving and taxes from your gross household income, you have a good grasp on what is available to spend—better known as *spendable income*. Now comes the fun part: establishing a plan for spending it how *you* want it spent. This is where your spending plan becomes a very freeing experience. You will no longer be flying by the seat of your pants, but will be planning your financial destination and using your available/limited resources to get you there.

Fill in all your expense items, using the spending plan form I've provided as a guide. You can download this form from my website at DrCorySFawcett.com. Enter something in every category. Don't say you won't need any new clothes and enter zero in the clothing category. You'll need new clothes, if not this year then next, and it needs to be a reasonably accurate figure.

In the various debt payment sections, including mortgage, car payments, student loans, etc., put in the minimum payment amounts.

For the savings category, put in the figure you will be saving to build your emergency fund—at least six months of living expenses. Don't include your retirement contribution in the savings category, because that is often taken out of your salary before you see it. If, on the other hand, the retirement contribution is coming out of the spendable income, such as a Roth IRA, then place it in the investment category.

Now total all the expenses and subtract this figure from the total spendable income to see what you have left. If the expenses are greater than the spendable income, expenses must be cut. Look back through the categories for areas where you might be overspending. You must cut back on expenses until money remains at the end of the month. This leftover money is what you will use to accelerate getting out of debt. Strive for a minimum of 10% of your spendable income. Only after establishing an accurate spending plan will you know how much discretionary income you have available for debt repayment.

Net Spendable Income - Total Expenses = Discretionary Income

For some of you, this exercise will be very enlightening. You now know the true cost of your habits. Maybe some of them are not worth what you are spending. Take a close look at what you spend and decide if you are spending your hard-earned money the way you want.

Are you getting the best bang for your buck? Would you be better off in the end to use some of that money to get out of debt, or improve your financial future in some other way? Do you have an expensive habit you can stop or change now to improve your situation, such as making coffee at home in the morning, rather than stopping at a drive-through on the way to work? Can you afford the house you live in? If not, start making changes now.

When my wife was a teenager, she used to compare every purchase to how hard it was to earn the money. Was buying this item worth five hours of babysitting? She knew what she went through to earn the money and wanted something of equal value when she spent her money. Do you do that? You know how hard you worked last month and how many days you took call. Is the car you're considering worth the effort you went through to earn the money? If you start thinking of your expenditures in this light, you will be less free about giving up your hard-earned cash.

Here is where the rubber meets the road. Now, rather than flying by the seat of your pants, you will regain total control. Cut the less important stuff and add the important. This is where Steven R. Covey, in his book *The Seven Habits of Highly Effective People* (Simon and Schuster), would tell you not to let the good things keep you from doing the great things. Make sure the great things have not been left out, and remove less important good things if needed.

If you don't have at least 10% of the total spendable income left as discretionary income after completing your spending plan, then some hard decisions need to be made. If the budget is that tight, expenses are too high to be supported by your income. There is not enough cushion to keep this plan out of trouble and comfortably pay off the debts. It's time to think about the big ticket items. The biggest problem areas for doctors are housing, automobiles, and recreation.

Many doctors have dreams larger than their income. Can your house be supported on your current income? If the total housing expenses exceed one-third of your spendable income, think about downsizing. Housing expenses include not only the payment but also the taxes, yard care, utilities, maintenance, internet, phone, insurance, and anything else attributable to the house.

The biggest problem I encounter when doctors are having money problems is a house they love but can't afford. This may be the entire problem with the spending plan. Moving to a less expensive house may free up enough money to have breathing room. Life is better when you can breathe.

Automobiles are another problem area. Is the auto section more than 10% of your spendable income? If so, this may be a problem.

These are the hardest decisions of all. Are there things in the plan that are too expensive? Now is the time to seriously take stock of this and make a spending plan with breathing room. Strive to have at least 10% of your spendable income available to pay off debt before going to the next step.

STEP FOUR: APPLY THE SNOWBALL METHOD

Treating your debt problem is very much like treating a cancer with chemotherapy. You look for the highest dose that will maximize the cancer kill and minimize the side effects. Honing in on a good spending plan is how you determine the maximum dose of money you can tolerate to reduce your debt, without suffering too many undue side effects. The discretionary income, calculated at the bottom of the spending plan form, is what you will use to get out of debt once and for all.

Many authors have written about the snowball method to pay down debt. I don't know where it originated. It is analogous to rolling a snowball off the top of a hill. As each debt is paid off, more money becomes available to pay off the next debt (the snowball picks up more snow), and so the debt payment amount increases—the snowball gets larger and larger and gains momentum as it rolls.

I paid off more than half a million dollars in less than six years using this method, as I described in my journey to becoming debt-free. So what I'm about to cover is not *theory*—it doesn't just *look good on paper*, and it is not something that will *work for me but not for you*. I did it myself and so have many others. It's not hard, it's not complicated, but you have to actually do it for it to work.

Medications do not work until they are swallowed.

Take the debts on your net worth worksheet and relist them in order from the smallest outstanding balance to the largest. This is the order you will use to pay them off. Like a magnifying glass focusing the rays of the sun to start a fire, you will focus all your available resources on one debt at a time. You will not be making extra house payments at the same time as you are paying off student loans. Make only the minimum required payments on all the debts except the one on which you are concentrating. This is the fastest way to get the snowball rolling.

PAY OFF THE SMALLEST FIRST

Some advisors would have you start on the loan with the highest interest rate. Others want the loan with the lowest balance-to-payment ratio to go first. In reality, you will be paying off your loans so quickly that it will make little difference which method you choose. Working from the smallest to largest loan also has the benefit of giving you faster results. It's the quickest way to retire the first loan and attain some momentum.

Add your discretionary income to the regular payment each month on only this first loan. Here is where the spending plan becomes crucial. You cannot make extra payments with money needed for something else in the plan, or you will get into trouble. Having money in the checking account doesn't mean it's available to spend on debt.

Concentrate only on the smallest loan, and pay only the minimum on all the other loans. If the regular payment on this first loan is $450, and you can afford to pay an additional $1,500, then the payment will become $1,950 each month. That's the $450 regular payment plus the $1,500 discretionary income.

Often, you can pay off the first loan in only a few months, even though you had planned on paying it over several years. I remember the excitement I felt when I paid off my first loan years ahead of schedule. I knew then and there the plan would work.

CELEBRATE YOUR MILESTONES

It's a good idea to have a reward established to celebrate the retirement of each debt. Maybe dinner at a favorite restaurant, a family picnic in the park, a trip to the beach, or whatever would be a true motivating reward for you. However, make sure the reward fits into your spending plan.

Now that the first loan is gone and you have collected your reward, add the $1,950 you were paying for that loan to the next smallest loan on your list. If the next loan has a $600 a month payment, add your $1,950 to it and begin making $2,550 a month payments. This loan will disappear very rapidly as well.

Keep up this pattern. Each time you pay off a loan, roll that total payment onto the next loan. The payment will increase with each loan. Usually the last loan on your list is your house, and it takes the longest to finish off. Maybe having a reward at each quarter mark for paying down the mortgage will work better than waiting a few years for the reward. Also, any extra influxes of money, such as bonuses or tax refunds, make a nice booster payment on the current loan.

Since there is a maximum amount of debt any given income can support, it will usually work out for everything to be paid off in less than seven years. With interest rates exceptionally low at the time I'm writing this, it's possible to borrow larger sums that need a little longer to pay off, if your loans are at the maximum your income will support. This seven years includes owning a house outright with no more mortgage! If it takes a little bit longer, that's OK. It's still much better to be done in eight or nine years than to take 30 or more to finish paying everything off. The money you save in interest will be going into your pocket and not your lender's pocket. If debts are not at your limit, you will be done much faster.

Now that you are well on your way to becoming debt-free, there are a few other things that can increase your momentum.

BUILD MOMENTUM
STOP ALL NEW BORROWING

Imagine a patient coming to the office with a nonhealing wound. They have tried everything, and nothing seems to work. You start them on the proper treatment and when they return next month, the wound still looks the same. How can that be?

When you ask the patient how things are going, you find they are scratching at the wound constantly. The wound cannot heal if they keep scratching off the epithelium as fast as the body is laying it down.

You also cannot pay off a credit card if you continue to add charges at the same time you are making extra payments. You must stop adding to your debt while paying it off. So stop borrowing money. If credit cards are a problem area for you, cut them up or freeze them in the center of a gallon block of ice, so you will have time to think about why you need to use credit while the ice thaws.

The next chapter will also list some other ways to save money to help build more momentum on your journey.

STOP BUYING NEW STUFF

One of the biggest complaints I hear about paying off debt is living on a shoestring. You absolutely don't need to scrimp to get out of debt, but if you choose to, it will speed things up. Continue to use the things you already have and don't buy any new stuff until you are debt-free.

A great example of this for me was the story I mentioned earlier about my stolen bicycle. We needed to replace it, and this would be the perfect time for my wife and me to get matching bicycles. Yesterday she didn't need a new bicycle, but today she suddenly does.

We didn't need to buy the second bicycle, yet I was ready to spend the money. My wife's question, "Are we debt-free yet?" became the slogan in our house for the duration of our quest to become debt-free. Every time I was tempted to buy something we really didn't need, she would ask me, "Are we debt-free yet?" That was all it took. She reminded me of our goal and I could then put off the purchase until we finished paying off our debt. After we made the last house payment, she couldn't use that line on me again. That's when I bought a convertible sports car. With cash. One of the many benefits of being debt-free.

During our debt repayment period, we never once felt deprived. We weren't deprived when we didn't buy the second new bicycle. We would have felt deprived, though, if we didn't replace mine and couldn't go on the family rides anymore. If you really must have something, look into estate sales. We were able to get a brand new bed, sheets, comforter, and frame for my son in college for the price of a new set of sheets.

By avoiding the purchases we didn't need, we had even more money available to pay down our debt. These little things add up. Bonus money, tax refunds, family gifts, and any other money we weren't counting on for our spending plan went toward the debt. You will discover, as we did after becoming debt-free, that you will be able to buy things with cash like never before in your life! Once you gain momentum, you may even decide to move some money from other categories for a while to speed up your debt elimination.

Buy only what you need. Postpone what you don't need.

Chapter 7

STAYING OUT OF DEBT

REASSESS THE SITUATION

You made it! You've joined the ranks of *doctors without debt*. What now? Certainly the first recommendation is don't borrow any more money, but there are others. Keep a close eye on your spending plan. Increase saving for future expenses, like your children's college and your retirement. Live life to its fullest, as you never know what might happen. Teach others what you've learned about the pitfalls of debt to save them from repeating your struggle. However, your debt-free story will not be as effective if you don't stay out of debt.

Now is a good time to kick back and take a moment to relish what you've accomplished. Most doctors don't own their home outright; they share ownership with a bank. You have joined a select group. Interest is no longer working against you, and as you convert from the getting-out-of-debt phase to the accumulating wealth phase, the real fun begins.

If you put yourself on a tight leash financially during the debt repayment period, loosen the reins a bit now. Increase spending a little and use some of the money the bank was charging in interest to enjoy life a bit more. Maybe take the vacation you put off or do something else to celebrate this great accomplishment.

This is a good time to revisit your spending plan. With no debt in the calculations, you can make some adjustments.

When we reached that point in 2001, we increased three expense categories substantially: giving, recreation, and investing. Those were the three areas needing a boost, especially the category of recreation. I like to play.

It's very important to avoid spending your money without a plan, or you might end up back in debt again. Your bank account will began to grow like never before. There's a big temptation when you see a large figure in the checking account to think it's time to buy something. Don't fall for that temptation. Rework the category amounts and come up with a plan for the money. Actively manage the money, stay in control, and stick to the plan.

WAYS TO SAVE

With a new spending plan in place, this is a good time to finish filling your six-month emergency fund, if it's not already full. Pushing it up to twelve months would be even better. The larger this account, the lower the risk that you will ever borrow money again. Be conscious of ways to save—don't blow the money. A penny saved is more than a penny earned. The penny saved isn't taxed.

STAY IN YOUR HOUSE

Houses are very expensive. The bigger the house, the higher the cost of upkeep. If you already own a house, you may be tempted to buy a bigger house when you become debt-free. If your house meets your needs, don't swap. The added expenses will require more of your income to pay the bills.

Changing houses also comes with a substantial transaction cost. When you add up all the costs of selling your current house and the costs of buying the new one, you will be astonished by the figure. So don't change houses just because you have more money available; you do not need the biggest house you can possibly afford. Stick to living in a nice house that meets your needs and is comfortable.

Look sometime at the ridiculous houses purchased by some of the rich and famous. How can you use 25 bedrooms? Why does anyone need a bowling alley in their house? Do you really need a personal racquetball court? It's very clear that having money creates a drive to spend it. Even to the point of buying things just to buy things. Don't fall into that trap. Be responsible with the new money available in your plan.

If you have not yet purchased a house, I believe now would be a good time to do so. Begin saving for the down payment and work out a payment amount that will nicely fit your plan—not the most you can afford. Also, examine your needs. Frankly, no one needs to live in a 12,000-square-foot house. The costs of upkeep will not provide you with an appropriate level of additional rewards. My wife and I toured such a house, and she commented about needing a riding vacuum to clean the place. Make your choices reasonable.

AUTOMOBILE EXPENSES

Automobiles are expensive. It's not only the purchase price and interest on the loan, but also the insurance, repairs, and upkeep that make them usually the second greatest expense in your spending plan. Americans have developed a love affair with their cars—an expensive love affair. I recently read a blog in which a new attending had accumulated more than $120,000 in car debt, with the purchase of his first two cars out of residency. He was asking for advice in the blog about paying off his student loans. He had some concern for them, but no concern about the car loans. He likes his cars, and I suspect they are going to drive him right into the poor house.

Today's cars have become quite reliable and safe. They also last a long time. There is no good reason to replace them every two years, yet many people do. You see an advertisement for the latest new car, which ignites a deep internal desire to have the latest thing. "Honey, did you see that car? Our car doesn't have Bluetooth capabilities like that one. I think we need to get a new car." There will always be a new gadget they are putting in the cars to entice you to replace the three-year-old fossil you are driving.

Don't become a victim of their advertising campaign. Drive your car until it becomes a problem, needs too many repairs, or no longer fits your needs. If you are still driving the two-seater you had when you were single, but now you have a family of three, you may need to find one that will meet your growing family's needs.

Try to avoid the need to purchase a brand new car, now that you are out of debt. Since it will last many years, a two-year-old car will be a great car and is purchased with a substantial savings over the new car price. The sports car I bought after we were debt-free was a dream goal of mine, and was purchased used. Now that you know better, buy your car from the person who needs one every two years.

CUT COUPONS

I know cutting coupons sounds silly for someone at the income level of a successful doctor, but think again. We recently vacationed to southern Florida. During that trip, we did the usual touristy activities we found in a travel brochure, which serendipitously contained several coupons. So if a boat ride around Key West costs $6 less per person by using a coupon, a family of four would save $24. If my income taxes are 40%, that's $40 I don't need to earn if I use the coupon. If it took me less than one minute to tear out the coupon, put it in my wallet, and present it at the time of purchase, that works out to $2,400 an hour ($40 x 60 minutes). Where else can you make that kind of money with almost no effort? Using coupons for things you were going to do anyway can save you a fortune. Don't pass up opportunities for free money.

REASONABLE VACATIONING

Vacationing tends to be a very expensive item in a doctor's spending plan. Nice vacations come in all sorts of cost ranges. There are lots of savings to be found in this category. Last year I took my family, plus one of my youngest son's friends, on a vacation to Disneyland. We were looking over the schedule and had one more day to fill. We had a choice to make: one more day at Disneyland or go to Universal Studios for a day. Since we already had a multi-day ticket at Disneyland, adding one more day was $25 each, or $125 total, before added sales tax.

To go to Universal Studios would be $95 each, or $475 total, before they add the taxes. So I asked the kids if we would really get $350 more fun by going to the other park for one day, not including the two-hour round trip drive across the valley, as we were staying a few blocks from Disneyland. They all agreed that playing one more day at Disneyland was the best option. That small choice of park for the day, taking into account my 40% income tax, was a difference of $585 in the amount I would have to earn to purchase the tickets, not including sales tax. Switching amusement parks would not provide $585 more fun. Another day at Disneyland was a blast. We will go to Universal Studios on the next trip to southern California.

There are many other ways you can take great vacations for a lot less money. Look into options that will give you what you are looking for—the same experience—for less outlay of cash. If you are looking for a relaxing time at a sandy beach, will you really be more relaxed on the French Riviera than lying on the sand in Florida for half the cost? Is the sun warmer in France? If you wanted to go to France to also see the Cannes film festival, then you will need to go to France. But if you just want to relax, save some money and relax at a less expensive alternative.

TAKE ADVANTAGE OF OFFERS

If you are like me, you get endless offers for deals. If they are something you would like, go for it. I have a credit card that generates frequent flyer miles for an airline servicing my town.

I put everything on the card and consequently have rarely paid for a flight in the last several years. I did not have to make any changes in my life to take the free flights. The lesson there is, don't leave free opportunities on the table.

MAKE YOUR OWN FOOD

I am surprised by how many people, who make a lot less money than I do, go out to eat every day for lunch. Eating out is expensive; you usually will eat too many calories, and the food will not always be healthy. If you pack a lunch for work, you can kill two birds with one stone. First, you will save a small fortune over your lifetime. Second, you will always be eating the food you want and it will be a much healthier diet. Save the eating out for a special occasion and don't make it an everyday thing.

Just how much can you save? Let's say you spend $9 every day for lunch when you go out. Bringing your own lunch from home might cost $3. You would save $6 each day. That's $30 a week, and for 48 weeks, that totals $1,440. Take into account your 40% taxes, and you will save $2,400 of earned income by brown bagging it. Who knows how many pounds you will save from your middle? For those of you who aren't fully investing in your 401(k), adding that $2,400 to your investments for 40 years at an average of 8% return would build your nest egg by roughly an additional $700,000. Withdrawing 4% per year comes to an extra $28,000 a year in retirement income. Not bad for simply choosing to eat better food.

OTHER WAYS TO SAVE

There are many ways to save money—to get out of debt faster or to use your money more wisely when you are debt-free. Have popcorn and a movie at home, recorded on your DVR, instead of going to the theater. Buy food in bulk at discount places like WinCo and Costco. Avoid designer labels for your clothing. Buy children's clothes at a secondhand store. Little kids don't wear out their clothes; they outgrow them. Make your own pizza at home instead of going out. Make your own coffee in the morning instead of using the drive-through. Let your conscience be your guide.

OPPORTUNITIES KNOCKING

I keep an account I refer to as my *opportunity account.* Traditionally, I kept about $50,000 in this account, in case an opportunity crosses my path. You never know what might come around the corner. If you have some cash available when someone approaches with a great investment, you can jump on it.

One day, I was approached by one of my partners with the idea of building a physician-owned surgery center. Getting the ball rolling meant purchasing a piece of property, and my portion would be $30,000. Because I had an account for just such a purpose, I could act quickly to complete the deal. Many similar deals have crossed my path over the years, and it's nice to be able to step up to the plate and not miss a golden opportunity.

As the project moved forward, the rest of the doctors in town were invited to participate. The initial offering called for $5,000. I was a fairly young doctor and, because of my opportunity account, I could act. Surprisingly, several physicians, who had been practicing many more years than I, did not have $5,000 readily available. There were many excuses. I have two kids in college, I just paid for my daughter's wedding, I just got back from Hawaii, I'm still paying my student loans . . . It was obvious to me the concept of an opportunity account was not commonly practiced.

I didn't understand how a doctor could be in practice for fifteen years and not be able to write a check for $5,000. Turns out many doctors live paycheck to paycheck. When I was younger, I didn't know that.

Once your spending plan is established, your debt paid, and your emergency fund is full, your financial life will usually be trouble-free. Life is good when you live within your means, and a whole lot less stressful.

If you want a bigger house, save some money and add it to the proceeds of the sale of your paid-off house to pay cash for the new one. Things you never thought were possible when you had a heavy debt load, are now well within your grasp. Life is very different when you have money in the bank.

I'm reminded of a joke I heard from Jeff Foxworthy, which I will poorly paraphrase for you. Bob had fallen behind in his car payments and couldn't understand why his car was being towed away by the repo man. What's the big deal? He was only a few payments behind. About six payments, to be exact. The repo man said he would be forced to tow the car away if Bob didn't pay something now. It would only take $1,000 to stop him from repossessing the car.

Bob said, "I don't have that kind of money. Who carries around that kind of money?"

The repo man said, "It doesn't have to be cash, I can take a check."

Bob's eyes gleamed with an idea, "Check, sure I can give you a check. Shoot, I thought you said you needed money. I got plenty of checks."

Having checks is not the same as having money. Having a credit card is not the same as having money. Now that you really do have money, keep it that way.

Chapter 8

BEGIN INVESTING

With lots of leftover money every month, now is the time to concentrate on building wealth. It's time to turn the tables on the bank and make compound interest work for you.

Investing is a very complex topic, and there are entire books written covering only this subject. But here are a few general points to help you get started. See the reading list on my website, DrCorySFawcett.com, for a list of helpful books on investing.

TAX-ADVANTAGED OPTIONS

Start by maximizing your tax-advantaged savings plans. Fill up the 401(k), IRA, HSA (health savings account), and any other available savings plan. These plans have a maximum contribution each year, and you should do your best to invest the maximum allowed. These are extremely advantaged accounts, so don't pull money out of them for any use other than to live on when you are retired. Pulling money out for a down payment on a house, for example, is a big mistake. You are saving that money for retirement, and using it for a house cuts back on your retirement funds—and with a limit on each year's contribution, you can't make it up. Once you pull the money out the first time, it will be easier to do it again.

The company retirement plan, such as a 401(k), is usually the best first place to put money. If you are lucky, your company will match some of your contribution. That is free money. Remember what I said about never passing up free money. Each year, invest the maximum amount you are allowed to contribute. When you get old enough for the catch-up provision, currently after age 50, the maximum amount you can deposit will increase. Keep contributing this new maximum. Your company retirement plan will have several options you can choose from; pick the option that best suits your risk tolerance. Usually the plan will offer free access to an advisor. Take advantage of this free service, and discuss how you wish to invest your funds.

The next place to put your money is an HSA. If you have a qualifying high-deductible health insurance plan, you can make before-tax contributions to your HSA. The 2016 limit on this contribution for a family is $6,750, or $7,750 if you are over age 55. This account will grow tax-free and if you take the money out for qualified health costs, you will never be taxed on the money. The thing to remember with this account is not to use any of the money until you are retired. If you leave this account alone and pay for your health-related expenses out of your current income, it will continue to grow tax-free, increasing your retirement nest egg. After you are retired and no longer have an earned income, then use the account for your health expenses.

The Roth IRA is the next place you should put your savings, if you still have money to invest after filling your company plan and your HSA. This currently has a limit of $5,500, or if you are over age 50, you can put in $6,500 per year. This account is for after-tax money, but the growth will never be taxed. Unfortunately, this is not available for everyone. In 2016, if you are married and filing jointly, you cannot contribute to a Roth IRA if your modified adjusted gross income (MAGI) exceeds $194,000.

The traditional IRA can be funded pre-tax, under certain circumstances, but you will pay taxes when you remove the money. This makes it less desirable than the Roth IRA, which has no tax when you take out the money. The traditional IRA will collect interest and capital gains without tax as it grows, until you withdraw the money. Both of the IRA types will charge a penalty if you withdraw the money before age 59 ½. But if you actually retire before age 59 ½, you can remove the money penalty-free using rule 72t, which allows you to set up a withdrawal plan without penalty if you follow their rules.

The backdoor Roth IRA is a clever alternative for those of you earning too much money to qualify for a Roth IRA. This takes advantage of the fact that a traditional IRA can be rolled into a Roth IRA at any time, and the income taxes owed on the growth of the traditional IRA will be payable at that time. You cannot already have a balance in a traditional IRA if you want to do this. To take advantage of converting your traditional IRA into a Roth IRA, you will make a traditional IRA deposit with after-tax dollars and then roll it over into a Roth IRA account immediately. With no growth, you owe no additional taxes. You have now made a contribution to a Roth IRA and the growth will never be taxed. Get some professional help the first time you do this, so you don't make a mistake and owe a bunch of taxes.

Another location to invest money in a tax-advantaged account is a 529 college investment fund. This money is saved for a child to use in college. The money will grow tax-free, and you will owe no taxes on it if it is used for education. State plans differ throughout the country, so check with your state for the rules. You are not limited to investing in your state plan—so if another state offers a better deal, go for it.

TAXABLE ALTERNATIVES

Any remaining investment money will likely end up in a taxable account of some sort—but I would like you to consider one more tax-advantaged place to put your money, and that is in rental real estate.

Rental properties are tax-advantaged. The government needs investors to help supply the population with housing, and they offer an incentive to do so. The incentive is called depreciation. This also creates passive income, which is important, as you will read in the next section.

For example, suppose you were to invest in an apartment complex costing $1.15 million. Subtracting $200,000 for the value of the land, which you cannot depreciate, the $950,000 remaining for the building value can be depreciated over 27.5 years. That means the first $34,545 of annual profit is tax-free, for the next 27.5 years. Depreciation is a great tax advantage, over most other kinds of investments in taxable accounts.

WHY YOU NEED PASSIVE INCOME

Active income is what you make by seeing patients and charging them for your services. If you don't work today, you don't earn any money today. Passive income is earned from operations you are not actively involved in, such as rental property income. Passive income still fills your bank account, even if you are sitting on the beach enjoying the sun in Hawaii. This can be your ticket to early retirement, if that is your goal. Once your passive income exceeds your living expenses, you no longer need to work for a living. Your investments will support you.

Rental real estate was the vehicle I chose to use as I began investing outside the tax-deferred vehicles. I was able to generate a passive income with real estate that was not dependent on my ability to produce. Passive income in taxable accounts is the key to an early retirement. Since retirement accounts generally will not allow you to withdraw the money in them without penalty before you reach age 59½, you can use the passive income from real estate to live on until you reach that magic age when you can begin to withdraw from your retirement accounts without penalties or restrictions. After twelve years of building my real estate portfolio, it was generating enough passive income to cover all my living expenses. That meant I was free to retire if I wanted to. This passive income can also allow you to withdraw less from your retirement accounts in the early years and let them continue to grow, tax-deferred.

DON'T BECOME A WHALE: EDUCATE YOURSELF

There are many other ways to invest. Be sure you fully understand what you are investing in and how you are making money. As doctors, we are a target for those who sell investments. We have a good income, and are often too busy to look into investments very closely. If, after being presented a new investment idea, you are not able to sum it up in one simple sentence, look for another investment, or learn more about this one before you invest. It's too easy to get caught up in the excitement of a great investment. It sounds so good. Almost too good to be true. Don't let the *get rich quick* bug get into your wallet.

This is important, so I'll say it again: never invest in something you don't understand. Investing should be simple. Beginning a simple plan and remaining consistent year after year will take you to financial independence much sooner than you ever realized was possible.

I'm sure you have heard of the TV show *American Greed*. I am amazed at how many people get caught up in an investment scheme they don't understand. Often the scammer says things like, "I know you don't understand this, but trust me." And money pours into the scam. The investors get greedy, see lots of dollar signs, and fall in line. They mortgage their house, take advances on their credit cards, and borrow from friends to invest as much money as possible in the opportunity. They sense they could *get rich quick,* and they jump right in.

Steady plodding brings prosperity.
Hasty speculation brings poverty.

This is not a new concept. That quote is written in Proverbs 21:5 and is part of a collection of helpful advice from a few thousand years ago by King Solomon. Is it possible the same scammers we see today on *American Greed* were around thousands of years ago? It looks that way. But this simple truth holds true today: steady plodding brings prosperity. You don't need to get risky or complicated. Keep investing in good, solid places and the money will grow and compound in your favor, which will lead to financial independence. You don't need to take risks.

When I first began investing, during my residency, I was maxing out my IRA and the residency 403(b) retirement plan. The 403(b) plan only had a few mutual funds to choose from, and I split my monthly investment into two mutual funds and let it ride. I could play with the money in my IRA a bit more, and play I did. I researched market timing and spent several hours each week learning about investing and watching my stocks on a daily basis. I figured I was a pretty smart guy, so I should be able to beat the market.

After a few years, I noted an interesting trend. The money I was actively trading and spending many hours on was not doing any better than the money put in a few mutual funds and left to grow untouched. Numerous reports stated that only 20% of professional investors—and I am not one of them—can actually beat the market in a given year. Next year it will be a different 20% of them who beat the market. If the professionals can't beat the market, what made me think I could?

Well, I can't. After I realized this, I stopped being an active investor/trader and became a passive investor. Now, I put my money into a mutual fund with a good track record, and let it ride. I no longer waste time watching the market and trying to beat it.

It's time in the market that counts, not timing the market.

I don't know who first penned this phrase but it holds true and I proved it myself. Learn from my experience and don't get fancy. Make sound, conservative investments you understand and do it every year. Invest the maximum amount your spending plan can handle. Keep as much as possible in tax-advantaged investments. It is not a hard formula. It's been proven year after year. If you follow this plan, you've got it made, so don't risk it.

Chapter 9

THE FINISH LINE

Finding yourself without debt draining away your wealth and a relatively high income is a nice place to be. Money begins to pile up, if you are not spending it all—and if you have been following my suggestions, you aren't. There will come a point where you realize you have accumulated more money than you need. Still, more is coming in and you begin to wonder, what's next?

I remember sitting in church one Sunday when the pastor preached a sermon on wealth. The take-home question was, "Do you have a finish line?" A place where you know you no longer need to be stockpiling more money for your future.

I had not been debt-free for very long at that time, and such a concept had never crossed my mind—a finish line for wealth accumulation. I was saving money and accumulating wealth as if that would be the plan for the rest of my life.

John D. Rockefeller, who was at one time thought to be the world's richest man, was once asked, "How much money is enough money?" He replied, "Just a little bit more."

The richest man in the world thought he didn't have enough and went on to accumulate more. Was I behaving in the same fashion? Was that the best approach? Is that all there is to life? Then I remembered a line from a children's book I used to read to my kids when they were small: *The Lorax*, by Dr. Seuss (Random House Books for Young Readers).

Near the end of the book, as the Once-ler kept getting wealthier by cutting down the Truffula trees and selling his products, and building a still larger empire, he said this:

And, for your information, you Lorax, I'm figgering on biggering

and BIGGERING

and BIGGERING

and BIGGERING . . .

Rockefeller didn't think he had enough, the Once-ler didn't think he had enough, and then the pastor got to the parable of the rich fool in Luke 12, where Jesus said: "Watch out! Be on your guard against all kinds of greed; a man's life does not consist in the abundance of his possessions."

And He told them this parable: "The ground of a certain rich man produced a good crop. He thought to himself, 'What shall I do? I have no place to store my crops.' Then he said, 'This is what I'll do. I will tear down my barns and build bigger ones, and there I will store all my grain and my goods. And I'll say to myself, "You have plenty of good things laid up for many years. Take life easy; eat, drink, and be merry."'"

"But God said to him, 'You fool! This very night your life will be demanded from you. Then who will get what you have prepared for yourself?'"

Wow! Maybe storing up enough for me and then kicking back to enjoy it is not the best plan.

If you set a finish line, at some point you will cross it. Then what will you do? Will you kick back and "eat, drink, and be merry"? You will have gained a lifetime of knowledge and skill. You will have an incredible ability to produce a large income you no longer need. Your knowledge and skill can still be put to good use. All too often, I see people retire to do nothing. They tend to just wither away.

I began to contemplate this notion of a finish line and what that would look like. It did make sense. What was the point of accumulating more than you need, when there are others in need? A steak can only taste so good. A house can only be so big and still be practical. You can only spend so much on a car and then things start becoming ridiculous. I sat down one night to come up with a plan that would create a finish line for me, in terms of wealth accumulation.

I developed a two-part finish line. First, I established a passive income goal I wanted to earn from my real estate ventures that would be more than enough to cover my needs. I had a spending plan and knew what my expenses were. I lived a very nice life on that plan. I had a nice house, three cars, a motorhome, and several weeks a year of time-shares to use; my kids' education was covered and we went on eight to twelve weeks of vacation each year. I could see little reason for me to spend more than what I was already spending on my lifestyle, for the rest of my life.

Second, I established a total amount of money to have in my retirement plans to cover me as a back up to the passive income. There it was, my finish line. There is no point sharing my numbers with you, as they will not be pertinent to your situation. You will need to come up with your own finish line. Once I passed those marks, there was no need for me to make a living. From then on, I could use my additional income to make a difference.

When I crossed my finish line, I told one of my partners I wanted to retire. He asked me what I was going to retire *to*. I didn't get the question initially. He went on to tell me of people he had seen retire over the past few years. The ones who quit because they didn't want to—or have to—work anymore were not as happy as they anticipated. Many of them went back to work again, after a short break. The ones who had a plan for their retirement did much better. They were retiring to something and not simply quitting their job.

He had a point. I had not formulated a plan yet, as to what I would do next. I was still relatively young with lots of productive years ahead. I kept working for two more years and began to work on a plan. I began to search for something else to do with my talents and abilities. I did not want to continue working at the fast pace I had been. The life of a general surgeon is busy and stressful. I wanted to slow down, but still be useful. But how?

Imagine that time in your future. You have passed the finish line. You have amassed a large stockpile of money and no longer need to produce an income to take care of your family. What will you do then? Do you love your work and want to keep working, and channel the income somewhere more useful than making your retirement plan even larger? Will you want to use your skills in a different fashion? Are you tired of doing what you have done all these years—do you want to shift your focus?

During the next two years, I looked for different ways to work that would be less stressful.

I began to work fewer hours and opened my mind up to some other ways to do medicine. I looked into doing some mission surgery in third world countries. I explored setting up a clinic at the nearby VA outpatient center to help veterans get set up for their colonoscopies. I looked into playing music professionally again, something I gave up during medical school and hoped that someday I would be able to return to. I set up a medical clinic in the local Gospel Rescue Mission, to see patients who had no physician. I started doing a radio call-in talk show monthly. Since I was no longer concerned with making a living, I was free to do some other things that didn't necessarily increase my income. This added a new dimension to my medical practice and spiced up my life.

I finally settled on what to do when I retired. I wanted to help the rural surgeons who worked alone. The town I lived and worked in had ten general surgeons. I lived within a few hours' drive of several towns that only had one or two surgeons. When these surgeons need a vacation, someone needs to fill in for them so the hospital can still operate normally. With my plan in mind, I announced my retirement from my practice of over twenty years.

I am now enjoying the slower pace of the rural towns. I am still doing surgery, and providing a needed function, keeping rural surgeons healthy and happy so they can continue practicing for many years.

With my slower schedule, I had more free time than ever before. I set out on a plan to help doctors with their personal finances and began to write *The Doctors Guide to* series of books. By thinking outside the box and wanting to be productive, I found things to do so I could make a difference in people's lives, now that my financial future was secure. I have established and passed the finish line, and I'm free to make a difference in a new way.

What are your special talents? What areas do you have an interest in pursuing that you were never able to do while you were busy making a living? There are many famous examples of people who finished one career and then started another.

Colonel Sanders began Kentucky Fried Chicken at age 65.

Laura Ingalls Wilder began writing the *Little House* series when she was 65.

Grandma Moses didn't begin painting until she was in her 80s.

Edmond Hoyle didn't begin writing about card games until around age 70.

Ronald Reagan was elected to his first public office at age 55.

Jimmy Carter worked with Habitat for Humanity after retiring from politics.

Dr. Ben Carson retired from neurosurgery and ran for President of the United States.

So what will you do if you find yourself in a position where you no longer need to make a living? Writing out the response to this question might even become a motivating factor to keep you on track to becoming debt-free.

Maybe you don't have any other special interests and want to keep on practicing medicine. That's great, since we will always need doctors and we currently are in a shortage. If you do keep working and generating a high income, and have crossed the finish line, you are in a position to become a philanthropist.

You will be in a position to direct the use of a considerable amount of money for causes you feel passionate about. You can financially help out a family member. Does the hospital need a new wing or special piece of equipment? Is the library in need of funding? Were you a Boy Scout and wish to help the local scouts in some way? Would you like to support a missionary? Maybe your college or medical school could use a scholarship fund? You could make it possible for a medical student to graduate debt-free. The possibilities are endless.

I had a conversation about this with one doctor who told me he had given a substantial portion of his wealth to a particular charity in his will. We talked about what the charity was doing to help the community. I asked if they needed any money now, and he said yes. Wouldn't it be better to give them your excess now, so you could enjoy seeing it used, rather than wait until you die? If you bequeath your money only after you die, is it really giving? You can't use it then anyway, and you won't see the good it produces.

Become generous with your excess while you are alive. Don't follow in the footsteps of people you read about, who made an absurd amount of money and then spent it on stupid things like a different color Rolls Royce car for each day of the week.

As a group, doctors are highly intelligent, driven, ambitious, and they get things done. What would happen in America if more doctors became debt-free and financially set for life? What could we do? How would the world become a better place? What would happen in rural America if more doctors were free to help? What would happen if all student loans were paid back well ahead of schedule and were available for the next generation to use? What would happen if we were giving abundantly to good causes?

Doctors have so much potential as a group. Much of that potential is being held back by debt. Over the last generation, doctors have become enslaved to their practices by the bondage of debt. It's time to get out of bondage and be free to achieve our God-given potential. Doctors without debt can become a movement of great momentum and power. Join me in reclaiming our greatness.

Bonus Material

At the end of my award-winning book *The Doctors Guide to Starting Your Practice Right,* I listed several plusses to becoming debt-free. I feel it would be good to repeat that list here, especially if you are not a new doctor and did not feel the need to read the first book in this series.

HANDLING YOUR MONEY WELL DECREASES STRESS—BIG TIME

Debt is a big stressor. Sometimes when you don't feel well, it's not clear how bad you feel until you are back to normal and can appreciate the difference. Becoming debt-free is similar. There were two points in my life when I noticed this phenomenon. The first was when I made my last student loan payment and the second was when I made my last mortgage payment. In both cases, I felt a great weight lifted off my shoulders that I didn't realize was there. Couldn't you use one less stressor?

REDUCING DEBT AND BEING DEBT-FREE GIVE YOU A VALUABLE ASSET . . . TIME

It's hard to imagine how much debt cuts into your free time. As it turns out, you feel a need to work more to pay off the debt. Many doctors don't go on vacation with their family, and instead stay home to work so they can pay the bills. You can feel free to take a day off during the week, or even an afternoon to go to a child's soccer game in a nearby city, when you don't feel the need to produce. The ability to take more time off, if you need it, will go a long way toward fending off burnout. Lower monthly expenses means a lower need to produce income, which means feeling freer to take time off with less guilt and worry . . . you get the picture.

RETURN THE MONEY FOR OTHERS TO USE

When you pay back student loans, that money becomes available for the next student to borrow. As tuition continues to rise, this may become a limiting factor. Now that you are earning a great living, pay the money back and let someone else use it. You don't need it anymore. They will be grateful for the opportunity, and society as a whole will benefit.

PAYING OFF DEBT GIVES YOU MORE DISPOSABLE INCOME

After paying off your debts, interest won't be charged against you. If you don't have to pay interest, that money will be available to you for some other use. If you are carrying $500,000 in debt with an average of 5% interest, that's over $2,000 a month in interest. Eliminating that debt gives you back the $2,000 a month to spend on other needs, plus the money you were paying in principal.

The bank doesn't deserve the money more than you do. Don't give away next year's income before you even have a chance to earn it. This increase in available money could be used for a better lifestyle, more investing for retirement, college money for the kids, better vacations, and the list goes on. What would you do with the extra $2,000 a month?

RETIRE EARLIER THAN YOU MIGHT OTHERWISE

You may love your job and want to work forever, but why not do it because you want to, and not because you have to? Getting out of debt gives you more savings and fewer expenses. An $800,000 mortgage requires an extra $2 million in savings to pay for it in retirement, if you are no longer working. Paying off the mortgage would mean retiring $2 million sooner. Then, if you want to continue to work, it will be on your terms. You never know how long your health will last.

MAKE A DIFFERENCE

When you are debt-free and have accumulated enough money so you don't need to work anymore, many other options open up for you. Now that you don't need to make a living, you can make a difference. What would you do if money was not a limiting factor? What kind of difference could you make in the lives of others?

How could the country be improved if droves of doctors were in such a position? Would you like to be in a position to substantially help your favorite charity? Maybe you can work in a third world country. You can help out at a critical access hospital in rural America, or work for the local homeless shelter, taking care of people who desperately need your help. The possibilities are endless.

GAIN NEGOTIATING POWER

The local hospital knows you need your income, so they have all the power in a negotiation. If a group of hospitalists want the hospital to make a change, but they are afraid of losing their jobs, they can be easily pushed around. If, on the other hand, all of the doctors were debt-free and no longer feared losing their jobs, they are in a position to say no to the hospital's demands. What a feeling, to be able to tell the hospital how it will be instead of the other way around.

If all doctors were in a position to walk away from a negotiation, they would have power. The hospital would be much more inclined to consider your way of thinking if you have some power at the negotiating table. Being debt-free gives you the confidence to stand up for your rights. If all of the doctors in America did this, what changes could we make in the healthcare system?

BE FREE AND HELP OTHERS CATCH THE VISION

Solomon stated in Proverbs 22:7 that:

> Just as the rich rule over the poor, so the borrower is servant to the lender.

Did you really go to school all those years to become someone else's servant? Another minion working for the bank? If you don't think you are a servant to the bank, skip a few mortgage payments and watch what happens. Debt removes a piece of your freedom. Once you escape from under the bondage of debt, many new opportunities will appear. You will benefit. Your family will benefit. The patients will benefit. America will benefit. Doctors without debt will be the ultimate win-win deal.

QUESTIONS? COMMENTS?

Dr. Cory S. Fawcett
DrCorySFawcett.com

I want to hear from you. Any feedback is welcome, and I want to know if you think I've missed an important topic, or you have a story to tell or found a mistake. Also, I didn't put everything I know into this book. Send me an email at DrCorySFawcett@gmail.com or contact me through my website at DrCorySFawcett.com.

If you found this book to be useful, please post a comment on my website. I'd truly appreciate it if you spread the word through social media or by posting a review on Amazon. Please pass on what you've learned to your colleagues.

Connect with Dr. Cory S Fawcett on LinkedIn

Like Dr. Cory S Fawcett on Facebook

Follow @drcorysfawcett on Twitter

Email DrCorySFawcett@gmail.com

Watch Dr. Cory S. Fawcett on YouTube

Acknowledgments

Many people contributed to the knowledge contained in this book. My parents, Jim and Wayna Fawcett, and grandmothers, Luella Fawcett and Virginia Brown-Petko, taught me valuable lessons about living within my means and saving for the future. My wife, Carolyn, whose catch phrase, "Are we debt-free yet?" was the inspiration for me to stay on track and complete my journey to becoming a debt-free doctor. Because of her I saved more, gave away more, and tithed more than I ever dreamed possible.

I would like to thank all of those who attended my Crown Financial Ministries small group discussions over the years. Your encouragement and willingness to change your lives for the better was an inspiration for me to bring this information to a larger audience.

A special thanks to those who did the test reading of this book and offered suggested improvement: J. Brant Darby, DDS;

Aaron Martin, DO; John Ermshar, MD; Owen Martin, DC; Marsha Evans; Maureen Feist; Danielle Conrardy, MD; Rob Bents, MD; Mark Thomas, MD; Nathan Kemalyan, MD, FACS; R. J. Leavitt, MD; Timothy M. Grant, MD, MBA, CPE; William Merbs; Allison J. Batchelor, MD, CMD; Sean Traynor, MD, FACS; my wife, Carolyn Fawcett; and my son, Brian Fawcett.

There are many others along the way who contributed to the information I learned and am now passing on to you. I'm sorry I can't list them all, or even remember them all, as they are too numerous to count.

Thanks to the team at Aloha Publishing, including Maryanna Young and Jennifer Regner, and the Fusion Creative Works design team of Shiloh Schroeder, Rachel Langaker, and Jessi Carpenter. Without them, this book would still be just an idea floating around in my mind.

About the Author

Dr. Cory S. Fawcett's passion for teaching personal finance spans his entire career. Through one-on-one counseling, as a Crown Financial Ministries small group discussion leader (a ten-week Bible study class on money management), and as a keynote speaker, he has been improving people's financial and professional lives for years. As an instructor for medical students and residents, he has found they have a hunger and need for financial wisdom and direction, as they transform into practicing physicians.

With his financial interest and background knowledge, he has served on several boards and financial committees throughout the years. He has been involved as owner, founder, or partner in more than two dozen business and real estate ventures.

The lack of surgeons in rural areas and his desire to work less led him to the decision to retire from his twenty-year practice, in a town with ten general surgeons, and assist in underserved areas. In February 2014 he began working part-time in rural Oregon towns with only one or two surgeons. With just one surgeon in town, the call burden of 24/7 availability is unsustainable. Dr. Fawcett provides them with a needed break from their pager, helping to keep rural surgeons healthy.

His current mission is teaching doctors to have healthy, happy, and debt-free lives—to regain control of their practice, their time, and their finances. He is writing, speaking, and coaching in an effort to improve the lives of his colleagues. Burnout, suicide, debt, and bankruptcy are increasing among physicians, dentists, optometrists, chiropractors, pharmacists, nurse practitioners, and others in the healthcare industry, and he focuses on halting the progression of these unnecessary outcomes.

Dr. Fawcett is an award-winning author, speaker, entrepreneur, personal finance coach, and now semi-retired general surgeon. He completed his bachelor's degree in biology at Stanford University, his doctor of medicine at Oregon Health Sciences University, and his general surgery residency at Kern Medical Center. After completing his training, he returned to southern Oregon to practice for twenty years in a single specialty, private practice group in Grants Pass. Since 1988 he has shared his home with his lovely bride Carolyn. They have two boys: Brian, who graduated from college with a degree in economics, and Keith, who is currently working on a degree in mobile development.

Made in the USA
Middletown, DE
27 March 2019